Where the Air is Wine
A Case Study of Sonoma County Wine Tourism

by

Michelle Renée Mozell

Where the Air is Wine:
A Case Study of Sonoma County Wine Tourism

Text Copyright © 2014
by Michelle Mozell
SSU Wine Business Institute
http://www.sonoma.edu/sbe/wine-business-institute/

This is a work of non-fiction. Names, characters, incidents, and dialogue are based on actual interviews with the participants as well as document analysis. The author represents that the data provided were formulated with a reasonable standard of care, and makes no representative or warranties, express or implied.

ISBN-13: 978-1499385243

ISBN-10: 1499385242

Where the Air is Wine:

A Case Study of Sonoma County Wine Tourism

Sonoma County Wine Tourism: The Marketing of Sonoma County, California.

The Unified Effort of Three Sonoma County Wine-Related Organizations to Market Sonoma County: Its Wine, Its History, and Its Natural Beauty.

by

Michelle Renée Mozell, Wine MBA Candidate
Sonoma State University Wine Business Institute
1801 E. Cotati Blvd, Rohnert Park, CA 94928
Email: mmozell@cox.net

Wine MBA Research Advisor
Dr. Liz Thach, Master of Wine
Sonoma State University, Wine Business Institute

"I ride over my beautiful ranch... The air is wine. The grapes on a score of rolling hills are red with autumn flame. Across Sonoma Mountain, wisps of sea fog are stealing. The afternoon sun smolders in the drowsy sky. I have everything to make me glad I am alive (London, 2014)."
Jack London, John Barleycorn, 1913.

"We wanted a place in the country, away not only from the crowded cities but winter weather too. I might as well admit that I'm one of those who goes for that 'it's-a-wonderful-place-to-raise-the kids' line... here we got more of everything we wanted...(Schulz, 2014)"
Charles M. Schulz, 1958.

"Sonoma County is truly one of the world's premier spots for growing and making great wines of all types, thanks to its ideal climate and varied terroirs. But it's the environment that surrounds those growing conditions that also sets Sonoma County apart - the natural beauty, ranging from coast to redwoods to mountains; the history and heritage; the agricultural diversity leading to a bounty of locally grown foods. Most of all, it's the people - a true community of growers, winemakers, and friends whose artisan passion makes Sonoma a place like no other
(Sonoma County Vintners, 2013 E)."

Table of Contents:

Summary

Sonoma County is a beautiful place. Spreading northward from the cool San Pablo Bay in the south, the county opens like a fan between the mountains in the east and the sea in the west, the crisscross of fertile, alluvial valleys filling the ancient streambeds of the region's three principal rivers and the narrow, soft-topped mountain ranges capped by woodlands of oak and madrone. Crafted by the intermittent tectonic interruption of the San Andreas Fault system, a constant scraping of the Pacific and North American plates just off the Pacific shore, the mountains merge into a crumpled landscape in the north. There, the evidence of the county's violent, volcanic past is evident as geysers pockmark the foothills of seismically inactive Mount St. Helena. (Sonoma County, 1994). The Pacific coast is rugged and rough, cold and difficult, with a series of spectacular escarpments, some reaching 1800 feet, spliced by "steep hills, marine terraces, sandy beaches, and off-shore sea stacks (Sonoma County, 1994)." Carpeting the coastal landscape are the Redwoods, heroically pointing heavenward from every hilltop and every ravine, the remaining old-growth groves finding protection within the massive cover of second growth forest. Inland, soft, oak-studded pasturelands give way to thousands of acres of meticulously manicured vineyards, the historic and economic lifeblood of the county. Though rarely too hot and rarely too cold to prevent the nurturing of premium winegrapes, the county's winegrape growers cling precariously each year to the potentially dangerous edges of its uneven, Mediterranean climate. A beautiful place, Sonoma County welcomed more than seven million visitors last year.

Sonoma County is a big place. Larger than the state of Rhode Island, the county is home to a half million residents. Along the Highway 101 corridor, the crucial north-south transportation lifeline that bisects the county, are the county's major cities - Santa Rosa, Petaluma, Healdsburg, and Cloverdale – spaced like jewels on a necklace. Today, the "101" is the vital artery connecting the San Francisco Bay area cities, only a 30 minute drive away, with this economic heartland. Off the "101," to the east and the west, are a galaxy of towns and hamlets that sparkle in the evening amid the pastoral expanse. And spaced within that array of towns, are the farms and vineyards that spurred the county's growth. Today, there are over 400 wineries and nearly 60,000 acres devoted to vineyard, many of which are multi-generational holdings (Carroll, 2014). With sixteen distinct and unique American Viticultural Areas (AVAs), the wine industry is a primary draw for many of those seven million annual visitors who collectively spend one and a half billion dollars a year.

But Sonoma County is a protective place: protective of its natural beauty, protective of its environment, protective of its open spaces, and protective of its economic vitality. Its towns and cities, though full of old history and invigorated by newly inspired efforts to revive and repair, are a testament to a populace seeking visitor dollars, but spurning an influx of new residents. Its farmers and grapegrowers fiercely protect their right to exist amid those towns and cities but, more vigorously, defend their historical right to a share of an ever-dwindling water supply. The wineries seek to protect their good name *and* their market share, toiling tirelessly to enhance both the quality and the price-point of their wines. The hotels and restaurants, the parks and museums, and the shops and the arts, all work to protect their portion of those visitor dollars, as well. And the residents, many of whom descend from native and settler families of centuries past, protect their right to the peaceful enjoyment of a legacy passed down to them, a historic heritage that is their birthright, while benefitting from the trickle-down of tourist spend. Sonoma County is a quiet and bountiful beauty sharing the annual influx of visitors from around the globe with its elegantly eclectic blend of environmentalists and entrepreneurs, artists and industrialists, shopkeepers and students, and, of course, its winemakers and grapegrowers.

Therefore, how does a county so rich, yet diverse, lure even more visitors to spend their dollars in its shops and wineries and restaurants and hotels? How might a county unify its message and, in a singular effort, seek an increase in annual tourist revenue? In Sonoma County, it is the "Trio," the unified promotional effort of Sonoma County Tourism, Sonoma County Vintners, and the Sonoma County Winegrape Commission, that has worked so successfully toward this end.

However, few would have predicted at mid-century the success that they found. Even two decades ago, each organization was in disarray. With no focus or common message, the county had what Tim Zahner, the Chief Marketing Officer for Sonoma County Tourism, calls a "parochial mindset (Zahner, 2014)." Hotels marketed for themselves; parks were running out of money; wineries and vineyards, both the fledgling and the age-old, generationally-passed, struggled. Times were tough and, it was discovered, a lack of organizational strength was to blame.

But now, times have changed and so have the marketing methods. So much so that in 2012, Sonoma County was named "the top wine destination" in the U.S. by TripAdvisor's Travelers' Choice Awards 2012 (Sonoma County Tourism, 2013 B) and, in the same year, Sonoma County was named one of National Geographic Magazine's "Best Trips (National Geographic Society, 2014)." Over the past few decades, the county's wines have been elevated to some of the best in the world. Its Pinot Noirs from the high, ridge-lined coast and the occasionally tempestuous Russian River stand tall with the best of Burgundy. Its Dry Creek Zinfandels are the envy of California. Its Rhônes and Bordeaux are coming of age. Truly, the wines of Sonoma are among the finest in the world propelling Sonoma County to a position among the great wine regions of the world. But Sonoma County offers so much more. Indeed, Sonoma County is a beautiful, bountiful place.

Introduction

Tim Zahner, Sonoma County Tourism's Chief Marketing Officer, sat at his desk, the mounds of paperwork and books and marketing material covered every square inch of his desktop. The windows behind him opened to the crystal-blue Sonoma skies. Even the parking lot was beautiful, serenely focused in the clear North Bay air: clean, crisp, with toned mellow light. This is what brings people to Sonoma County: beauty, serenity, quiet. Even on days that ought not be beautiful, Sonoma County is beautiful. Tim sat down for the interview, somewhat tired, appearing thin from what could be the result of his continuous travels to fulfill his enduring pledge to emplace more (and more) visitor "heads in beds." This is a sale made much simpler by marketing a magnificent spot on the globe that, also, happens to make transcendent, beautifully-crafted wines. Tim is a tireless pitchman for the county, always composed, yet delightfully and entertainingly animated and articulate. True to form, within moments of sitting, he sprang up once again to provide a half-hour tour of the new offices for the "Trio," the "pet name" for the three Sonoma organizations now working together to promote the sustained growth of the full complement of Sonoma County tourism: its hotels and restaurants, its parks and beaches, its wines and vineyards, its families and its workers. Tour completed, he returned to his desk. He sat back, arms behind his head, and answered, when asked, that his biggest concern, after all of his organization's marketing success, is getting too big.

Karissa Kruse, the President of the Sonoma County Winegrowers, met for her interview at Starbucks, the din and the clang of the pots and the whirring of the coffee machines were as fast-paced as her life, it seems. She traipsed all over the county promoting Sonoma Grapes. Bouncing from meeting to meeting, she has been warmly received by her organization and its members. Rarely ceasing to market their grapes and to protect their livelihoods, they love her here. She chugged down her coffee quickly, but talked even faster. Everything in her life these days, one could imagine, is kind of a blur, as she shuttles from place to place, giving speeches, supporting and setting up conferences, meeting with County Supervisors and a host of other stakeholders. She is a whirlwind of activity. She tirelessly supports this county and loves this county; she loves what she is doing. She is a staunch supporter of the growers, their families, the community, and the future of the land itself. Even this interview had to be cut into two as she just accepted at the last second an opportunity to guest speak at a local radio station's wine-focused broadcast. Under her leadership, the organization has grown. But, when asked, she is quick to point out that keeping a reign on that growth, keeping it in focus and in check, so as to manage that growth, is always a concern.

Sara Cummings, the Director of Communications at Sonoma County Vintners, sat behind her desk, piles of paper neatly stacked on her desk. Nothing seemed out of place. Though it is Honore Comfort that heads the organization, it was Sara who met for the interview. She was dressed beautifully, but somewhat subdued, and she spoke calmly, assuredly, as though something inside was at rest. Devoted to her position and to her charge - the promotion of Sonoma County wines and the livelihood of its vintners - she, with the quiet dignity of assured belief, spoke of the honorable perseverance and integrity of its wine-crafting community, of the region's long journey toward achieving international renown, approval, and respect. As the artisan of the organization's words of promotion, she spoke proudly and eloquently of that achievement. Yet, when asked, she was quick to point out that though success breeds success and continued success means continued growth, with over half of the county's 400 wineries participating as members to date, the organization is not seeking an increased share. To Sara, unchecked growth is a problem. Delivering value for those wineries participating is the true key to success. Growth can hinder that delivery of value. Sitting forward, chin atop her folded fingers, elbows resting firmly upon her desktop, Sarah smiled, then sighed, confessing that though she is looking forward to retiring one day, she still has a heart for Sonoma County wine: "there is much to do in terms of educating consumers, the media, and trade about Sonoma Count and its wines." She begins, "What would you like to know?"

Sonoma County:

An Introduction to Sonoma County

Blessed with extraordinary natural beauty and a climate abundantly well-suited to the wine industry, Sonoma County produces some of the world's finest wines.

Sonoma County is the largest and northernmost of the nine San Francisco Bay Area counties. In 2010, its population was 483,878. The city of Santa Rosa, with 167,815 residents, is its largest city and county seat (California State Association of Counties, 2014). Comprising 1,768 square miles (California State Association of Counties, 2014), larger than the state of Rhode Island, Sonoma County stretches from the Mayacama Range in the east, which separates the county from neighboring Napa County, to the rugged Pacific Ocean coast in the west. In the cool south, the silty flatlands meet the cold San Pablo Bay. In the very warm north, the landscape is furrowed by intermittent rows of mountains and valleys running, in general, southeast to northwest.

Climatically, the prevailing weather systems and wind come from the Pacific Ocean, so areas closer to the ocean and on the windward side of higher elevations receive more autumn rain through the spring and more summer fog (Sonoma County Winegrape Commission, 2013 A). Places further inland, and particularly those areas east of significant elevations, tend to experience moderate rain shadow, thereby receiving less rain and fog in the summer (Sonoma County Winegrape Commission, 2013 A). The coast is typically cool and foggy throughout the summer with high temperatures in the mid to upper 60s; the inland valleys, especially the further north the location, experience much warmer temperatures and a drier climate (Sonoma County Winegrape Commission, 2013 A).

Agriculture and tourism are two major drivers of Sonoma County's economy. Climate, soil and elevation are key factors in abundant agricultural production levels. Agricultural production, lead by wine grapes, reached record highs in 2013, as grape production soared. In all, more than seven million visitors come to the county each year to taste the wine and experience the natural beauty and recreation opportunities in Sonoma County (County of Sonoma, 2013 A). As grape and wine production increased, so, too, did wine tourism numbers. In a recently released report, Sonoma County's wine industry brought an economic impact of $13.4 billion in 2012. This includes providing 54,297 full-time equivalent jobs, directly and indirectly, from winegrowing and winemaking in Sonoma County (Carroll, 2014)." Currently, Sonoma County has the sixth lowest unemployment rate among California Counties (Wilkison, 2013) at "5.7 percent in December, down from a revised 6.0 percent in November 2013 as the jobless rate continued to decline to levels not seen since the summer of 2008 (Brown, 2014)(see figure 1)." Despite the economic malaise following the last recession, Sonoma County employment projections from the State of California's Employment Development Department show that total employment in the county is expected to increase nine percent between 2008 and 2018, with approximately 16,700 new jobs over ten years (County of Sonoma, 2013 B), many of them tourism-related positions.

Figure 1: Sonoma County Unemployment Trendline
(Source: Wong, 2014).

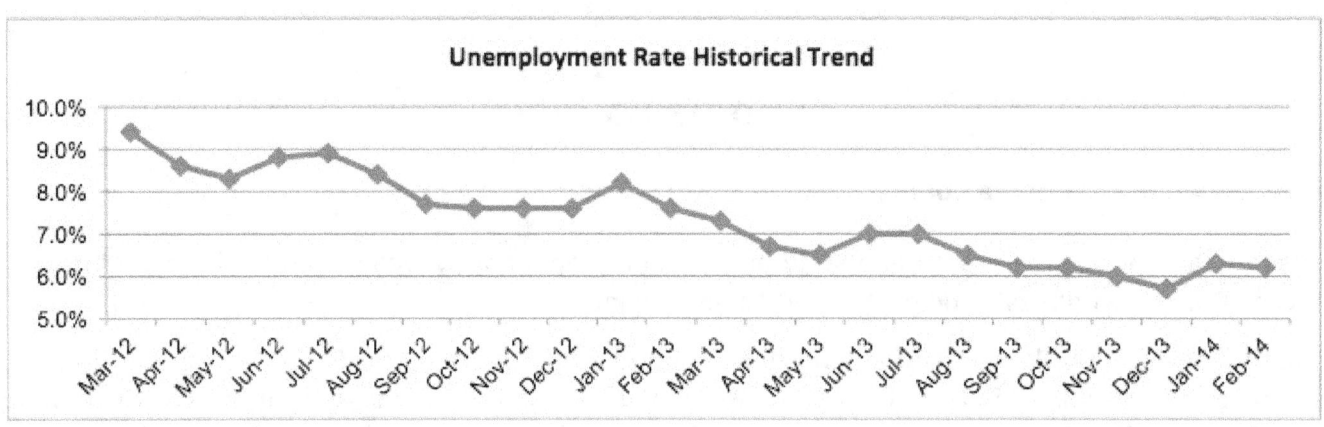

An Overview and Brief History of Sonoma County Wine

It is believed that grapes were first planted in Sonoma County at Fort Ross, the Russian outpost on the Sonoma coast, in 1812. But no one is quite sure. It is well known, however, that "Mission" grapes were planted by Spanish Franciscan Father Jose Altamira at Mission San Francisco Solano in Sonoma in southern Sonoma County in the early nineteenth century, the first historical record of winegrape plantings in the county. From there, viticulture spread as cuttings were carried throughout the northern California to initiate new vineyards. By mid-century, wine grapes were an established part of agriculture in the region (Sonoma County Vintners, 2013 A).

In 1855, Agoston Haraszthy, a gregarious and "larger-than-life" Hungarian native, the self-proclaimed "Count of Buena Vista (Buena Vista Winery, 2012)," purchased the Salvador Vallejo vineyard in Sonoma Valley northeast of the town of Sonoma. He renamed his vineyard, Buena Vista. (Recently purchased by the sprawling wine empire of Jean-Charles Boisset, Buena Vista is the oldest working winery/vineyard in California [Buena Vista Winery, 2012].") Haraszthy, rapidly emerging as the chief proponent of California wine, was commissioned by the California legislature in 1861 to study the viticulture of Europe. Following his European venture, he returned to California with more than 100,000 cuttings of premium European winegrape varietals (Sonoma County Vintners, 2013 A). As his plantings flourished, he continued to passionately promote California wine, eventually being honored by many as the "Father of California Viticulture (Pinney, 1989)." Following the development of Buena Vista, up until the time of Prohibition, many wineries were established in Sonoma County, such as Foppiano, Korbel, Simi, Sebastiani, Gundlach, and Bundschu (now Gundlach Bundschu) (Sonoma County Winegrape Commission, 2014 C). Many exist to this day.

In the 1920s there were 256 wineries in Sonoma County, with more than 22,000 acres in production (Sonoma County Vintners, 2013 A). However, Prohibition greatly impacted Sonoma County's winegrowers: commercial winemaking faltered, with many vineyards turned over to other crops (such as plums). Upon the repeal of Prohibition in 1933, fewer than 50 wineries in the county survived. Even as late as the 1960s, only 12,000 acres were planted to winegrapes (Sonoma County Winegrape Commission, 2014 C). However, as American wine consumption grew, more and more vineyards were planted. As winemakers came to realize the potential to craft extraordinary, world-class wines from Sonoma-grown grapes, the number of wineries began to multiply, as well.

Today, there are more than 400 wineries and 59,218 acres of vineyards within sixteen American Viticultural Areas (AVAs) (Carroll, 2014). Zahner and Cummings are quick to point out that there are even more this year. According to the Sonoma County Winegrape Commission, "There are dozens of multi-generational growers and winemakers in the county (Carroll, 2014)." Yet, despite the advance of time, many vineyards are, to this day, owned and operated by small producers and growers, many of which are multi-generational, family-owned farms. In fact, forty percent of all the vineyards in the county are less than 20 acres and a full eighty percent of all vineyards are less than 100 acres. Winegrape production remains, to a great degree, a family farm activity. According to the Sonoma County Winegrowers, "No other California region can match Sonoma's heritage and continuing commitment to that heritage (Sonoma County Winegrape Commission, 2014 A)." The combination of history, authenticity, family farming, sustainability, and diversity in topography, climate and soil all contribute to world-class wines (Sonoma County Winegrape Commission, 2014 A).

Sonoma County currently is divided into sixteen American Viticulture Areas that, according to the Sonoma County Vintners, "reflect the wide variety of climate and soil conditions in the county, the large production in the County, and the prominence of Sonoma County in the wine market (Sonoma County Winegrape Commission, 2014 A)." Differences in soil and climate mean cooler climate grapes, such as Pinot Noir and Chardonnay, grow well in certain regions and other grapes, such as Syrah and Grenache, grow in the warm weather sites. In Sonoma County, each AVA is significant, displaying very well understood regional distinctions in wine expression.

As listed by the Sonoma County Vintners, the following are appellations in Sonoma County (Sonoma County Winegrape Commission, 2013 B):

Alexander Valley: 15,000 vineyard acres and 42 wineries. Earned AVA status in 1984.

Bennett Valley: 650 vineyard acres and four wineries. Earned AVA status in 2003.

Carneros: 8,000 vineyard acres and 22 wineries. Earned AVA status in 1983.

Chalk Hill: 1,400 vineyard acres and four wineries. Earned AVA status in 1983 (w/revision 1988).

Dry Creek Valley: 10,000 vineyard acres and 50 wineries. Earned AVA status in 1983.

Fort Ross – Seaview: 506 acres and five wineries. Earned AVA status in 2012.

Green Valley: 3,600 vineyard acres and ten wineries. Earned AVA status in 1983.

Knights Valley: 2,000 vineyard acres and two wineries. Earned AVA status in 1983.

Moon Mountain: 1,500 vineyard acres. Earned AVA status in 2013.

Northern Sonoma: 329,000 acres. Earned AVA status in 1990.

Pine Mountain – Cloverdale Peak: 230 vineyard acres. Earned AVA status in 2011.

Rockpile: 150 vineyard acres. Earned AVA status in 2002.

Russian River Valley: 15,000 vineyard acres and 70 wineries. Earned AVA status in 1983.

Sonoma Coast: 2,000 vineyard acres and seven wineries (excluding wineries in Russian River, Green Valley, Carneros, and Chalk Hill). Earned AVA status in 1987.

Sonoma Mountain: 800 vineyard acres and three wineries. Earned AVA status in 1985.

Sonoma Valley: 14,000 vineyard acres and 55 wineries. Earned AVA status in 1981 (amended in '85 & '87).

Sonoma County produces a wide variety of grapes sourced from regions all over the world, including, but not limited to, France's Burgundy, Bordeaux, Rhône, Loire, and Alsace; Italy's Tuscany, Piedmont, and Veneto; Germany, Portugal, Spain, and Austria. Chardonnay leads the way, closely followed by Pinot Noir, Cabernet Sauvignon, Sauvignon Blanc, and Merlot. The Sonoma County Agriculture Commissioner released these totals for 2011 and 2012 (Office of the Ag Comm, Sonoma County, 2013):

Figures 2 and 3: Sonoma County Winegrape Production, Annual
Source: (Office of the Ag Comm, Sonoma County, 2013)

Winegrape Production

Red Varieties	Year	Acreage Bearing	Acreage Non-Bearing	Total	Tons	Production $/Ton	Total Value
Cabernet Franc	2012	662.3	2.4	664.7	1,906.5	$2,325.46	$4,433,500
	2011	655.9	6.7	662.6	1,568.6	$2,209.15	$3,465,300
Cabernet Sauvignon	2012	11,904.5	119.4	12,023.9	47,194.0	$2,313.56	$109,186,200
	2011	11,726.8	291.5	12,018.3	33,126.8	$2,111.24	$69,938,700
Carignane	2012	610.4	0.0	610.4	510.6	$1,879.74	$959,800
	2011	615.4	0.0	615.4	373.2	$2,019.14	$753,600
Malbec	2012	330.7	68.3	398.9	2,469.2	$2,284.02	$5,639,800
	2011	322.4	76.6	399.0	1,110.5	$2,340.51	$2,599,200
Merlot	2012	5,137.2	1.0	5,138.2	21,627.6	$1,496.57	$32,367,300
	2011	5,126.6	23.4	5,149.9	14,670.5	$1,380.85	$20,257,800
Meunier	2012	123.5	0.0	123.5	581.2	$2,735.16	$1,589,700
	2011	108.5	15.0	123.5	301.4	$2,698.80	$813,500
Petite Sirah	2012	587.9	10.5	598.4	3,149.1	$2,424.27	$7,634,300
	2011	575.0	22.2	597.1	2,521.1	$2,325.25	$5,862,200
Petite Verdot	2012	210.7	0.6	211.3	1,162.6	$2,669.78	$3,103,900
	2011	209.2	2.6	211.8	851.7	$2,461.02	$2,096,100
Pinot Noir	2012	12,077.5	144.9	12,222.4	52,793.2	$3,014.62	$159,151,500
	2011	11,862.6	377.1	12,239.7	28,350.2	$2,902.47	$82,285,700
Sangiovese	2012	91.0	36.5	127.5	1,341.5	$2,270.04	$3,045,300
	2011	89.5	36.5	126.0	845.2	$2,204.51	$1,863,300
Syrah-Shiraz	2012	1,785.0	4.7	1,789.7	5,252.2	$2,148.20	$11,282,800
	2011	1,773.1	19.1	1,792.3	3,614.0	$2,124.31	$7,677,300
Zinfandel	2012	5,243.4	54.2	5,297.6	21,204.2	$2,419.54	$51,304,500
	2011	5,216.8	81.1	5,297.9	13,101.0	$2,357.61	$30,887,100
TOTAL REDS	2012	38,763.9	442.4	39,206.4	161,709.9	$2,453.74	$396,794,100*
	2011	38,281.7	951.7	39,233.4	101,818.5	$2,301.97	$234,383,200*

* Revised from 2011

Winegrape Production

White Varieties	Year	Acreage Bearing	Acreage Non-Bearing	Total	Tons	Production $/Ton	Total Value
Chardonnay	2012	15,989.4	313.7	16,303.1	81,581.6	$1,893.66	$154,487,900
	2011	15,424.1	895.2	16,319.3	52,374.4	$1,843.94	$96,575,300
French Colombard	2012	35.6	0.0	35.6	116.6	$544.74	$63,600
	2011	35.6	0.0	35.6	86.3	$519.38	$44,900
Gewürztraminer	2012	135.0	0.0	135.0	640.0	$1,543.11	$987,600
	2011	135.0	0.0	135.0	220.1	$1,451.86	$319,600
Muscat Blanc	2012	16.7	13.0	29.7	101.6	$1,837.13	$186,700
	2011	16.7	0.4	17.0	40.2	$2,062.50	$130,000
Pinot Blanc	2012	51.6	1.0	52.6	368.8	$1,728.41	$637,500
	2011	45.1	6.4	51.6	185.8	$1,730.81	$419,900
Pinot Gris	2012	476.2	1.5	477.7	2,701.0	$1,661.48	$4,487,700
	2011	476.2	1.5	477.7	1,422.7	$1,635.34	$2,326,600
Sauvignon Blanc	2012	2,475.9	98.3	2,574.2	17,159.4	$1,418.49	$24,340,500
	2011	2,425.6	142.4	2,568.1	8,886.0	$1,368.74	$12,162,700
Semillon	2012	127.4	0.0	127.4	470.9	$2,063.69	$971,800
	2011	127.4	0.3	127.7	437.0	$2,298.45	$1,004,500
Viognier	2012	244.3	0.0	244.3	843.5	$2,251.74	$1,899,400
	2011	241.8	1.5	243.3	361.4	$2,282.41	$824,900
White Riesling	2012	32.7	0.0	32.7	363.8	$1,864.34	$678,300
	2011	37.2	0.0	37.2	206.4	$1,944.56	$401,400
TOTAL WHITES	2012	19,584.8	427.5	20,012.3	105,351.7	$1,811.93	$190,890,000
	2011	18,964.8	1,047.7	20,012.5	64,800.3	$1,784.38	$115,628,400*
TOTAL WINEGRAPES	2012	58,348.8	869.9	59,218.7	267,061.6	$2,182.80	$582,942,100
	2011	57,246.4	1,999.4	59,245.8	166,618.8	$2,083.08	$347,080,300*

* Revised from 2011

9

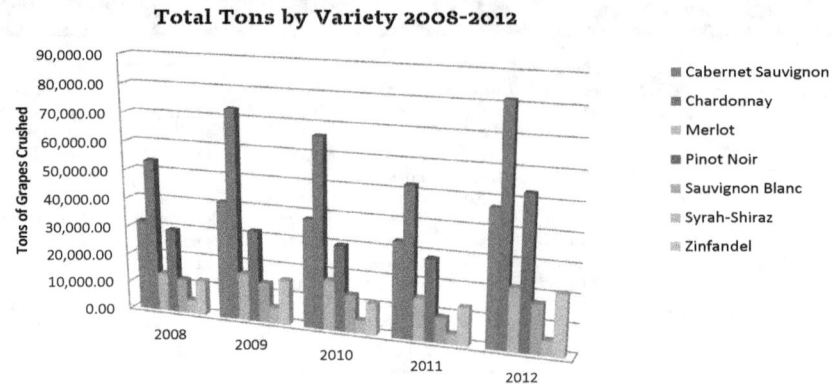

An Overview of the California Tourism Industry

Travel is one of the world's largest industries. In the United States, it contributes a hefty share to our gross national product, as well. According to the US Travel Association, in 2013, "travel and tourism" delivered $2.1 trillion to our economy and "supported 14.9 million jobs, including 7.5 million directly in the travel industry and 6.9 million in other industries (US Travel Association, 2014)." Travel-generated payroll for those employed in the U.S. travel industry was $209.5 billion. One of nine non-farm jobs is created directly or indirectly by the industry and it is among the top ten industries in forty-eight states in terms of employment (US Travel Association, 2014).

In 2013, $855.4 billion was spent directly by domestic and international travelers in the United States, an average of "$2.4 billion a day, $101.4 million an hour, $1.7 million a minute and $28,154 a second (US Travel Association, 2014)." This activity spurred an additional $1.1 trillion into other industries and directly generated, for local, state and federal governments, $133.9 billion in tax revenue. At nearly 2.7 percent of the nation's gross domestic product, its economic effect is widespread: each U.S. household would pay $1,093 more in taxes without the tax revenue the industry generates (San Diego Tourism Authority, 2014). Additionally, travel may be considered the number one service we "export (San Diego Tourism Authority, 2014)."

In California, the industry is an economic driver, as well: total direct travel spending in California was $109.6 billion in 2013. $12.5 billion in tax revenues is generated by that direct travel spending, equivalent to $970 dollars of tax revenue for each household in the state. About 60 percent of this revenue is generated by the travel spending of international visitors and residents of other states (Dean Runyan and Associates, 2014). The industry's contribution of $51.6 billion in 2013 represents about 2.5 percent of total California GDP (Dean Runyan and Associates, 2014).

According to VisitCalifornia, "the multi-billion dollar travel industry in California is represented primarily by retail and service firms, including lodging establishments, restaurants, retail stores, gasoline service stations, and other types of businesses that sell their products and services to travelers (Dean Runyan and Associates, 2013)." During 2012, travel spending in the California increased by 4.5 percent. In real dollars, travel expenditures rose by 2.3 percent from 2011 to 2012 and 1.7 percent the preceding year (Dean Runyan and Associates, 2013). In that same year, "travel spending in California directly supported 917,000 jobs, up 2.8% from 2011, while earnings increased by 4.9% over last year, at $32.3 billion. This is the second consecutive year of employment growth following the recession (VisitCalifornia, 2014 A)." The 917,000 travel-generated jobs delivered by the industry in 2012 are still below the 929,000 jobs supported by travel in 2008 (CITE 1). Nevertheless, for every $1 million spent in California by domestic and international travelers, nine jobs are created (Dean Runyan and Associates, 2014) (see Figure 5).

Figure 5: California Direct Travel Spending Impacts Upon Employment and Earnings
Source: (VisitCalifornia, 2014 B)

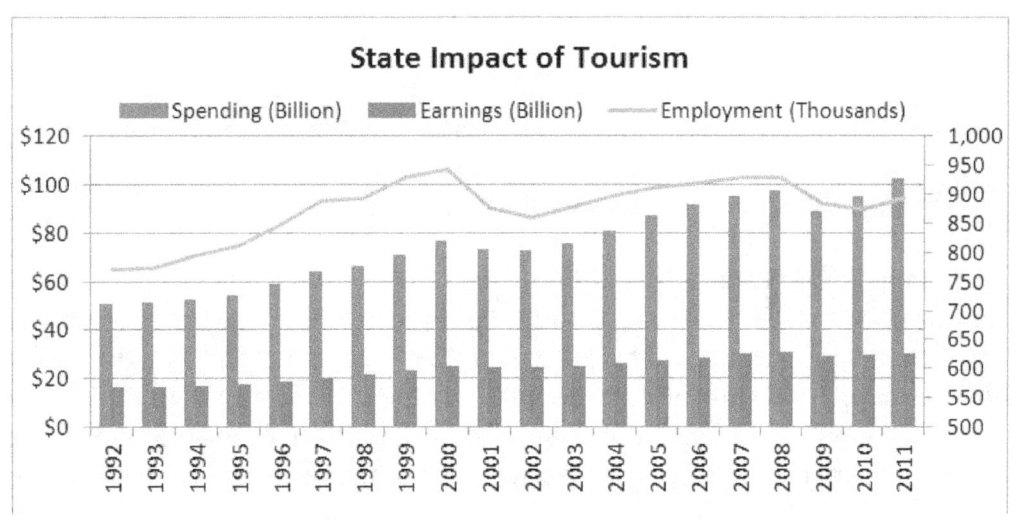

California continues to be a high-demand destination for both domestic and foreign travellers. In 2012, 215 million domestic "person-trips" (defined as a visitor trip made to a specific location) were recorded (San Diego Tourism Authority, 2014). This provided California with the largest market share of domestic travel of all states with a 2012 share of 10.82%. Of the 215 million trips to California, 51.59 million (24%) came from outside California. California's leading out-of-state domestic markets were Arizona, Nevada, Texas, Washington, New York, and Oregon in 2012 (VisitCalifornia, 2014 A).

6.4 million overseas travelers visited California in 2012, which represents a 21.5% share of all overseas travel to the United States (VisitCalifornia, 2014 A). Foreign visitors spent nearly $12.9 billion in California that year. California's leading overseas, non-North American, visitor markets in 2012 were: China (not including Hong Kong), the U.K., Japan, Australia, and Germany (VisitCalifornia, 2014 A)).

Mexico led all visitors with nearly 7 million visitors to California in 2012 and 1.54 million visitors came from Canada. (This total is 6.8% of all Canadian travel to the US) (VisitCalifornia, 2014 A).

Tourism's tax impact continues to represent a very healthy percentage of government tax receipts. Local tax revenues, generally the county-collected Transient Occupancy Tax (TOT), rose by 7.8 percent driven by increased lodging tax receipts due both to room demand and room rates (Dean Runyan and Associates, 2013). However, state travel-generated tax revenue dropped slightly due to a reduction in the state sales tax rate (Dean Runyan and Associates, 2013)). (See Figure 6)

Figure 6: California Transient Occupancy Tax by Jurisdiction
Fiscal YearAmounts in $1000
(Dean Runyan and Associates, 2013)

	*Rate	2003	2004	2005	2006	2007	2008	2009	2010	2011	2012	2013
SONOMA COUNTY												
Unincorporated	9.0%	5,284.5	5,212.8	5,672.1	6,269.7	7,253.4	7,784.1	7,456.8	7,284.3	7,929.6	8,902.8	10,100.7
Cloverdale	10.0%	21.0	47.5	76.2	105.6	139.0	164.3	164.9	142.7	145.0	144.3	161.3
Healdsburg	12.0%	880.3	905.6	972.7	1,163.7	1,635.8	1,862.4	1,669.1	1,595.4	1,928.0	2,209.1	2,418.3
Petaluma	10.0%	881.1	1,066.9	1,198.5	1,373.1	1,446.7	1,482.1	1,312.2	1,154.3	1,321.3	1,471.2	1,680.8
Rohnert Park	12.0%	1,364.7	1,368.2	1,447.4	1,435.4	1,773.7	1,863.5	1,755.9	1,637.6	1,747.7	1,940.5	2,202.9
Santa Rosa	9.0%	3,093.5	3,036.0	3,236.5	3,589.8	4,178.7	3,972.5	3,317.6	3,057.9	3,237.4	3,606.5	4,144.6
Sebastopol	10.0%	238.2	233.2	252.7	249.5	338.2	318.6	226.2	213.4	269.8	300.9	332.6
Sonoma	10.0%	1,695.5	1,899.3	2,047.9	2,310.1	2,439.2	2,613.2	2,200.1	1,979.2	2,211.4	2,508.1	2,661.2
Windsor	12.0%	0.0	216.8	422.2	541.3	688.1	752.7	917.6	1,068.0	1,209.1	1,285.0	1,425.8

An Overview of US and California Winegrape and Wine Production

Wine is produced in all fifty US states. According to the Wine and Vines Magazine, the total number of wineries in the United States in 2014 reached 7,762. Of these, 6,565 are produced by bonded wineries with a physical location, whereas the other 1,197 are created by virtual wineries (Wine Communications Group, 2014). A "virtual winery" is "described as an organization with its own management and winemaker, but without a bonded facility, that produces and bottles at least one wine brand using the services of a bonded facility of another organization (USDA, 2013)." California currently accounts for a 47% of all US wineries with 3674 wineries in production. The next five states with the largest number of wineries are: Washington with 689, Oregon with 566, New York with 320, Virginia with 223, and Texas with 208 (Wine Communications Group, 2014) (see figure 7). Every year wine production in the United States increases, especially in California. Statistics from the United States Department of Agriculture's Statistical Service recorded a record-breaking 2013 California harvest.

Figure 7: Wineries in the United States
Source: (Wine Institute, 2014)

Bonded and Virtual Wineries	
Type of Winery	Number of Wineries
U.S. Bonded[A]	6,565
U.S. Virtual	1,197
U.S. Total	7,762

[A] Bonded winery premises counted within this chart (figure 6 above) include every licensed production facility of single firms or individuals, licensed warehouses, experimental wineries and wineries with no case goods production or fermentation capacity. Bonded winery licenses are issued by U.S. Tax and Trade Bureau for the purpose of designating a tax-paid environment for wine (Wine Institute, 2013 A).

As an industry, wine is an important commodity. US wine consumption has grown steadily over the past four decades. The growth in US sales can be attributed to many factors, including the increase in the quality of American wines, the opening of markets, and the elimination of trade barriers within the global marketplace. "Among the key growth drivers are favorable demographics, a widening consumer base and increasing points of distribution in both on- and off-sale outlets," such as Starbuck's new retail wine-by-the-glass and the online efforts of Amazon.com and Facebook Gifts (USDA, 2013).

The Wine Institute reports, "Wine shipments to the U.S. market climbed by nearly fifty percent since 2001 and it is likely that American consumption will continue to expand over the next decade as wine continues to gain traction among American adult consumers"; today, "the U.S. is the largest wine market in the world with 19 consecutive years of volume growth (Wine Institute, 2014)."

California wine grape production is cyclical, primarily due to shifting patterns of weather and climate. Some years the climatic conditions provide a bountiful harvest, and other years, such as 2010 and 2011, crops are low. However, yields in 2012 and 2013 were extraordinarily large, with 2013 exceeding the record 2012 total yield (USDA, 2013). According to the Wine Institute, "Vintners and growers throughout California reported another high quality and generous vintage in 2013. Following a warm and dry spring with near ideal conditions for bringing grapes to maturity, harvest was remarkably smooth and wineries are at capacity and working with some very high quality winegrapes (Wine Institute, 2013 B) (see figure 8)."

Chardonnay grapes led the way in the 2013 California harvest. According to the USDA, in 2013, "Chardonnay accounted for the largest percentage of the total crush volume with 16.1 percent. Cabernet Sauvignon accounted for the second leading percentage of crush with 11.2 percent of the total crush. The next eight highest percentages of grapes crushed included wine and raisin grape varieties (USDA, 2013)." Zinfandel comprised 10 percent of the total with Merlot following at 7.4 percent (USDA, 2013).

Figure 8: California Wine Grape Production
Source: (USDA, 2013)

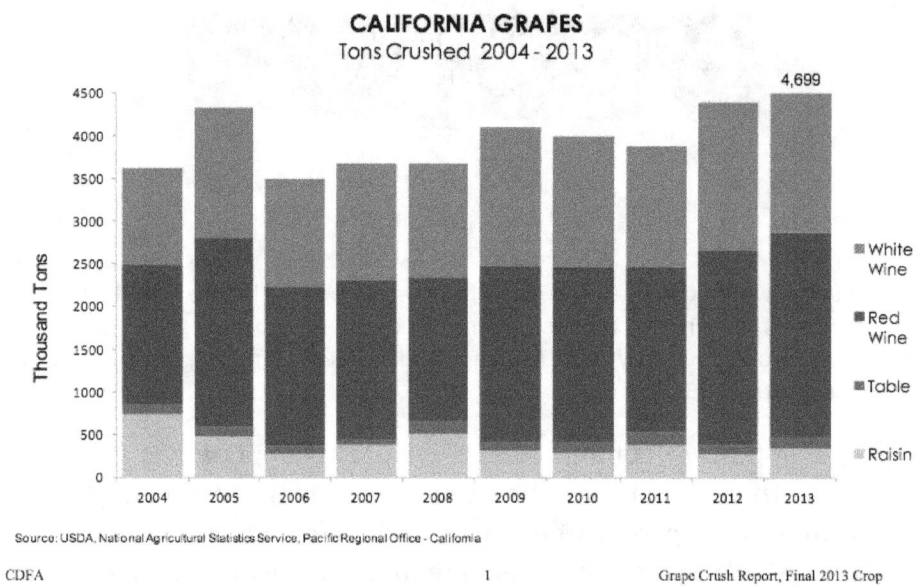

CALIFORNIA GRAPES
Tons Crushed 2004 - 2013

Source: USDA, National Agricultural Statistics Service, Pacific Regional Office - California

CDFA   1   Grape Crush Report, Final 2013 Crop

An Overview of Sonoma County Wine Tourism Industry

Sonoma County Tourism proclaims, "Tourism and wine are big business in Sonoma County (Sonoma County Tourism, 2014 B)." This is very true. Yearly, more than seven million visitors come to Sonoma County spending nearly 1.5 billion dollars: almost $300 a night in lodging alone (Sonoma County Tourism, 2014 B). "Tourism doesn't just affect tourism business, it affects everyone from farmers in Petaluma to grocers in Santa Rosa to public safety around the county (Sonoma County Tourism, 2012)." This influx of revenue is important: it supports more than 17,000 local jobs and adds almost $100 million to tax coffers, vital income to the government, that is used for "government revenues, and those funds are used for general funds for government, regional parks, arts and cultural organizations, affordable housing, and public safety (Sonoma County Tourism, 2014 A)" (see Figure 6 above).

According to Sonoma County Tourism, that annual "visitor spend" goes into three primary tills: lodging, (the "classic" motel/hotel), restaurants, and to other various local merchants. However, from there it "spreads rapidly as the employees get paid and spend on good and services locally; so there is this nice 'multiplier effect' as a result of tourism (Sonoma County Tourism, 2012)."

Dr. Robert Eyler, Professor of Economics and Director of the Center for Regional Economic Analysis at Sonoma State University, classifies tourism an "export industry," a service that Sonoma County *exports* to those that come here (Sonoma County Tourism, 2012). He explains with the example of a winery's tasting room seeking to "push out" their product, their wine, as far as possible to consumers who are not locals, consumers who will consume their product elsewhere (Sonoma County Tourism, 2012). The tasting room, he explains, is meant solely to "draw people in from the outside as they leave their money here. They take the service, then, they go away. It has the same, exact multiplier economic effect on the local economy as if your were manufacturing something and selling it worldwide (Sonoma

14

County Tourism, 2012)." As local cheese-maker, Liam Callaghan, adds, "Tourists are word-of-mouth marketing. Visitors are taking their experience that they have found here in Sonoma County with our incredible products and experience we have here and taking it home. The person talking about their experience with their friends: there is nothing more powerful than that (Sonoma County Tourism, 2012)."

Tourism, especially wine-related tourism, is a primary driver of the county's economy.

A Brief Introduction to the Three Sonoma County Wine Organizations/Associations

The force behind the continuing success of the marketing of Sonoma County are the three primary Sonoma County wine-tourism-related organizations: Sonoma County Tourism, Sonoma County Vintners, and the Sonoma County Winegrape Commission, known, collectively within those organizations, as the "Trio." They are:

Sonoma County Tourism: According to Sonoma County Tourism, "Sonoma County Tourism (also known as SCT) is the official destination marketing organization dedicated to promoting Sonoma County as an overnight destination (Sonoma County Tourism, 2014 A)."

Sonoma County Winegrape Commission: According to the Sonoma County Winegrape Commission, the "Sonoma County Winegrape Commission, dba Sonoma County Winegrowers (SCW), was established in 2006 as a marketing and educational state government agency dedicated to the promotion and preservation of Sonoma County as one of the world's premier grape growing regions. With more than 1,800 growers, SCW's goal is to increase awareness and recognition of the quality and diversity of Sonoma County's grapes and wines through dynamic marketing and educational programs targeted to wine consumers around the world (Sonoma County Vintners, 2013 B)."

Sonoma County Vintners: According to Sonoma County Vintners, "Sonoma County Vintners (SCV) is the leading voice of Sonoma County wine, dedicated to raising awareness and building understanding of Sonoma County as one of the world's premier wine regions, noted for its heritage of artisan winemaking, distinct growing regions, and extraordinary quality. Founded in 1944, SCV represents more than 200 wineries and affiliates of all sizes throughout the county (Sonoma County Vintners, 2013 B)."

An Introduction and History of Sonoma County Brandmark

By the end of the century's first decade, the "Trio," sought to "add power and efficiency" to the branding of Sonoma County and Sonoma County wine. To do so, they initiated a process to "conjunctively label" Sonoma County so as to "increase recognition of Sonoma County as a place with world-class wines, abundant agriculture and premium visitor experiences (Sonoma County Winegrape Commission, 2014 B)."

The Trio defines "Conjunctive Labeling" as the "unified labeling of a wine to show both region and sub-region (AVA) of origin (as well as) the inclusion of 'Sonoma County' on the label of all Sonoma County wines along with any AVA designation (Sonoma County Winegrape Commission, 2014 B)." The purpose of the conjunctive labeling project was threefold: 1) "to build brand equity for Sonoma County wines and preserve and strengthen Sonoma County's position as a recognized world-class wine region"; 2) "to increase sales of wines produced from Sonoma County grapes," and 3) "to increase recognition for every AVA within Sonoma County, both well-known and less familiar, and ensure that consumers understand where they are (Sonoma County Vintners, 2013 C)." The Trio adds, "Businesses in the areas of wine-making, winegrowing and agriculture and tourism are encouraged to adopt the brandmark and use it within the licensing guidelines to promote the genuine, authentic and independent nature of Sonoma County's brand (Sonoma County Winegrape Commission, 2014 B)."

From this effort, the "Sonoma County" brandmark was created as part of that unified branding campaign. And, from this effort, the "We Are Sonoma County" branding effort emerged (Sonoma County, 2014). (See Figures 9 and 10).

Figures 9 and 10: The Sonoma County Brandmarks
Source: (Sonoma County, 2014)

Sonoma County Tourism

An Introduction to Sonoma County Tourism, The Organization

Sonoma County Tourism (SCT), a private, non-profit 501(c)(6) organization, markets itself as "the official destination marketing organization dedicated to promoting Sonoma County as an *overnight* destination (Sonoma County Tourism, 2014 A), italics mine)." Chief Marketing Officer, Tim Zahner, continually stresses that the goal of SCT is to fill as many beds in as many Sonoma County hospitality-oriented businesses as possible, an effort he labels as "heads in beds (Zahner, 2014)."

A destination marketing organization, a "DMO," is an organization specifically designed to promote its specific geographic destination, whether that be a region, a town, a city, a state, or a country, with the primary purpose of increasing the number of visits to its destination by tourists and business travellers. Typically DMOs encourage tourism by branding and marketing the destination's "product awareness" to business travellers and tourists (Destination Marketing Association International, 2014)." By doing so, the DMO helps bring visitor spending to its destination and, thereby, helps secure the region's economy. According to the Destination Marketing Organization International (DMOI), the purpose of a DMO is to "increase the economic benefits of tourism and meetings to their respective destinations, inspire travelers to visit their destination, influence travel throughout their communities to increase spending and enhance the visitor experience, and attract conventions, meetings and events to their destination (Destination Marketing Association International, 2014)." DMOs "come in many different forms, but all are the principal organization of a given political division or subdivision that is organized to promote its respective destination to attract visitors and/or to solicit and service conventions (Destination Marketing Association International, 2014)." A DMO's primary "audiences" are "vacation and leisure travelers; meeting professionals, convention attendees and business travelers; and tour operators and travel agents (Destination Marketing Association International, 2014)." Annually, "DMOs produce billions of dollars in direct and indirect revenue and taxes for their destinations' economies with their marketing and sales expertise (Destination Marketing Association International, 2014)."

Organized originally in 2001 as the Sonoma County Lodging Association, SCT began as a collaboration of the county's tourism industry and the public sector "to formulate ideas and investigate ways of creating a funding structure to support a comprehensive tourism marketing program … to support and increase the vitality of this industry sector. In these discussions, the idea of creating a special countywide tourism business improvement area (BIA) emerged (Sonoma County Tourism, 2014 A)." By 2005, SCT became "the lead organization advocating the development of a new business improvement area (Sonoma County Tourism, 2014 A)."

Today, "with a staff of sales, marketing and public relations, communications, and administrative professionals," STC markets primarily "to three main markets: individual leisure travelers, meetings and groups, and 'tour and travel' (the buyers of packaged travel like tour operators and travel agents). Combining these three segments provides a 'balanced portfolio' of potential travelers," so that SCT can continue to effectively deliver upon its charter: bringing more "heads in beds" to Sonoma County (Sonoma County Tourism, 2014 A).

Duskie Estes, co-owner of Zazu Restaurant and Black Pig Meat Company in Sebastopol, admiringly declares, "SCT is not a big bureau of unknown faces. It is real people who go out into the community and try to get people involved and try to have their pulse on what is going on. They are real people working really hard to promote Sonoma County (Sonoma County Tourism, 2012)."

Tim Zahner, Sonoma County Tourism Chief Marketing Officer

Tim Zahner has been with SCT since 2006. He is the organization's Chief Marketing Officer. According to Zahner, his chief obligation is to "oversee the branding and marketing of the organization to their customers, as well as the crafting of the messaging and marketing strategy to stakeholders (Zahner, 2014)." He is, also, in charge of and responsible for communicating with "*our* segments of leisure travel (e.g., non-meetings and non-group tours) and individual travellers that come to our website (Zahner, 2014)." Since he came on board, the organization has grown from "six or seven" employees to twenty-three employees. Despite that growth, Zahner states, "We are made to be 'lean.' We always want to be program-rich and staff-poor. We are non-governmental and this is good. It permits us to hire good managers and work efficiently with vendors (Zahner, 2014)."

According to the SCT website, Zahner's past positions have been with the San Francisco Convention and Visitors Bureau (now San Francisco Travel); the Franciscan Missionaries of Our Lady: Haiti Mission, Inc.; the Hunger Task Force of Milwaukee; the Institute for Wisconsin's Future; and freelance travel and news writing (Sonoma County Tourism, 2014 E).

A History of Sonoma County Tourism

Tim Zahner introduces the bumpy history of SCT with an allegorical footnote into the movie, *A Beautiful Mind*. In the film, John Nash, the brilliant mathematician made famous by the movie, advances his adaptation to modern "Game Theory," a theorem known as the "Nash equilibrium." Game theorists "use the Nash equilibrium concept to analyze the outcome of the strategic interaction of several decision makers. In other words, it provides a way of predicting what will happen if several institutions are making decisions at the same time, and if the outcome depends on the decisions of the others. The simple insight underlying John Nash's idea is that one cannot predict the result of the choices of multiple decision makers if one analyzes those decisions in isolation. Instead, one must ask what each player would do, *taking into account* the decision-making of the others (Schelling, 1980)."

Zahner explains, "In the late nineties, different cities and different regions did not 'play' well together. We had a delightful Bohemian spirit here in the county where every city wanted to do everything their own way; there wasn't a huge amount of working together. At the same time, a group of hoteliers were looking at the problems of funding mechanisms (for a unified marketing operation in Sonoma County) (Zahner, 2014)." Cities and regions, as well as visitor centers, hotels, and restaurants, competed independently *with* each other. There was no unified marketing effort. "We were in disarray." At the same time, the county was collecting taxes (the Transient Occupancy Tax, or TOT), distributing money to each independent visitor center that, in turn, used the money to market *only* for *their* region (Zahner, 2014).

As an example, Zahner posits, "If two restaurants compete without speaking with one another and simultaneously compete for the same diners, each can go out there and advertise: One will try everything it can do to try to lure that diner and the other restaurant will try everything it can. They can drop prices, do specials, copy each other, but there is kind of a 'race to the bottom' that occurs. There can be a 'solution' where one can win and the other can lose, a 'solution' that is the reverse, but the restaurants are not getting to a situation that is a kind of 'optimal equilibrium' where both are kind of winning and are both happy enough. What Nash proposed in his equilibrium was the idea that to assure the best outcome, both parties need to agree as to how they are going to compete and what outcome they are going to 'go with' so to arrive at the best possible outcome for everyone (Zahner, 2014)."

"Essentially, what we needed to do as a region and as an organization was to agree as to how we were going to compete and how we would find the right audiences for all of us. I hear from Ben Stone, who runs the EDB (the County Economic Development Board), that the whole 'thing' came to a head when all these visitor centers were pointing fingers. The county finally said to Ben, 'This is now your project (Zahner, 2014).'"

"So, in the nineties, we decided we needed to work together. Ben had the wisdom to recognize that the 'dirty little secret' in this business: governments are not very good at marketing. Simply, governments are not made for that. Instead, he had the wisdom to 'spin this out' and with the assistance local hoteliers, businesses, and visitor centers, he created a new organization. And by 2005, through several shifts, it was from these different, competing forces that Sonoma County Tourism, a private, non-profit 501(c)(6) organization, came to be. And with it a funding mechanism and we became the organization created solely to promote Sonoma County (Zahner, 2014).

Tim stepped in in 2006.

The official history, however, as presented on SCT's website, follows (Sonoma County Tourism, 2014 A):

> "In March 2001, leaders in the tourism industry and the public sector began to formulate ideas and investigate ways of creating a funding structure to support a comprehensive tourism-marketing program. In these discussions, the idea of creating a special countywide tourism business improvement area (BIA) emerged.

The Sonoma County Lodging Association (SCLA) became the lead organization advocating the development of a new business improvement area. In 2004, SCLA promoted the development of the business improvement area to its members, community leaders, public officials and tourism-related organizations. In November 2004, SCLA saw their vision become reality when the Sonoma County Board of Supervisors established the Sonoma County Tourism Business Improvement Area (SCTBIA).

Soon after the establishment of the SCTBIA, the organizational framework for the Sonoma County Tourism Bureau (SCTB) was developed, including articles of incorporation and by-laws. In addition, the five-member SCTBIA Advisory Board was established, as well.

On Jan. 1, 2005, a new era in funding Sonoma County tourism marketing began as the SCTBIA went into effect. The development of the new Sonoma County Tourism Bureau took a significant step forward in February 2005 as the 22-member board of directors

In June 2005, the Board of Supervisors ratified a contract with SCTB to market Sonoma County and promote overnight visitors. On July 1, 2005, the SCTB officially became the destination marketing organization for Sonoma County."

Sonoma County Tourism: The Organizational Structure

According to the SCT website, SCT is "a private, non-profit 501(c)(6) organization, staffed by professionals in the fields of sales, marketing, communications, and administration. It is governed by a volunteer board of directors, with input from committees, stakeholders, and the general public (Sonoma County Tourism, 2014 A)."

The IRS defines "a private, non-profit 501(c)(6) organization" as "an organization whose purpose is to engage in a regular business of a kind ordinarily carried on for profit, even though the business is conducted on a cooperative basis or produces only sufficient income to be self-sustaining. Its activities are directed to the improvement of business conditions of one or more lines of business rather than the performance of particular services for individual persons... which are not organized for profit and no part of the net earnings of which inures to the benefit of any private shareholder or individual (Reilly, 2003)."

Tim Zahner has coined the term, "Marketing Federalism," to describe how SCT is governed and functions. Essentially, SCT is a private, non-profit 501(c)(6) organization governed by a 22-member Board of Directors. Thirteen members of the Board are selected annually and the Sonoma County Board of Supervisors selects the other nine members.

By statute, SCT reports directly to a committee within the County Board of Supervisors. The county, since SCT's transition into a 501(c)(6) organization, contracts with SCT, Zahner states, "for those dollars they give us, the Transient Occupancy Tax (TOT) dollars. Every November, therefore, we have to tell them what we have done with the money and what we are going to do with the money in the coming year. We are not county employees. No one in this office is a county employee, but we do meet regularly with them every two months (Zahner, 2014)."

The Board members are divided into five committees: Executive, Finance and Legal Committee, Governance and Human Relations, Public Relations and Marketing, and Group Business Development. The Board's incoming Chairperson is Pauline Wood, the President of the Petaluma KOA. The SCT Board hires the SCT staff (including Tim Zahner in 2006). Two County Supervisors, Efren Carillo and Mike McGuire, sit on SCT Committees.

When describing the SCT staff organization, Zahner describes it as "a little flattish" because there are just three departments all at the same level of the organizational scale: Public Relations, Marketing, and Partnerships; Meeting, Group Sales, Tour and Travel; and Finance (Zahner, 2014). Zahner is the Chief Marketing Officer "on par," he says, with the Chief Financial Officer, Bill Judson, and Chief Sales Officer, Mark Crabb, all of whom fall under the oversight of CEO, Ken Fischang. The CFO, due to statutory fiduciary duty, reports to the Board of Directors, as well (Zahner, 2014).

Sonoma County Tourism: Organizational Stakeholders and Customers

Customers:

The SCT website states, "SCT's efforts are divided into three main segments of travelers: individual leisure travelers, meetings and groups, and 'tour and travel,' which are the buyers of packaged travel like tour operators and travel agents. Combining these three segments provides a 'balanced portfolio' of potential travelers, so SCT can bring more 'heads in beds' throughout the year (Sonoma County Tourism, 2014 A)."

Tim Zahner's explanation of customer segmentation is an insightful illustration of how a DMO operates. According to Zahner, SCT has four "classes of customers" and thirteen "audiences." He has personified each audience with a make-believe character, each with a name and a photo that become part of his staff meeting's conversation. "In a way it is easier to identify customer segments by assigning to each category of customer a name and a face," Zahner explains. "My team sits down and talks about our different audiences. Who are we targeting? I deliberately made the groups look more and more diverse because America is that way. America and Sonoma County are turning either older and grayer or younger and browner (Zahner, 2014)."

Zahner's four "classes of customers" and the associated "audiences " are (Zahner, 2014):

1) People who are coming to Sonoma County to spend the night. Clearly SCT's most important mandate is to fill the county's hotel beds, therefore, Zahner concludes, "the most important customer is an overnight visitor." Fitting into this category are:

"Michael, the Boomer Man and Mary, the Boomer Woman."

"Bert and Carolyn, the Gen-Xers."

"Sienna the Millennial."

"George the Silver Voyager."

"Kim, the Foodie."

"Alex, the International Traveler."

"Dan, the Gay Traveler."

"Amy, the Bride."

2) People who *influence* people who are coming Sonoma County to spend the night. Much of SCT's sales and marketing effort is geared toward convincing a tourism-related decision-maker to choose Sonoma County for a visit and, of course, an overnight stay. Fitting into this category are:

"Nancy, the Meeting Planner."

"Wendy, the Wedding Planner."

"Clyde, the Tour Operator."

"Sandy, the Travel Writer."

3) The Partners who are "part of the organization." This class consists of the hotels, wineries, restaurants and other businesses that are both part of the organization as well as its customers. The tourism-related businesses of Sonoma County are entitled to the services of SCT just for being located within the County. Zahner continues, "Some, at first, think it is a trick; but somehow I believe I should charge $25 or so because people value something more if they pay for it." Fitting into this category is but one character:

"Pierre, the Partner."

4) The County Government. Zahner reiterates, "Governments are not made to do this type of activity. They are not very good at doing county promotion. We're nimble, we're fast. They are our customer because we are using their name (Zahner, 2014)."

Stakeholders:

To Zahner, stakeholders are quite similar to customers. In fact, he sees much overlap. To Zahner there are five primary categories of stakeholders (Zahner, 2014):

1) Customers. Zahner sees this group as his "'Number One' stakeholders."

2) All tourism-related businesses. This category includes, essentially, every business and other interest that SCT represents.

3) All allied organizations. With particular importance are the two other organizations within the Trio, the Sonoma County Vintners and the Sonoma County Winegrowers. Others include the AVAs, the regional and state parks, and other governments.

4) The residents of Sonoma County. To Zahner this is a "big stakeholder for whom there are huge impacts, including an annual $1.47 billion economic impact, so our residents are clearly a stakeholder for both good and for bad. Our residents, as stakeholders, that have legitimate concerns about tourism. But all that money goes to General Funds in a lot of cities and this is great. It helps cities and counties with housing, public safety, and parks."

5) Our elected officials.

SCT strives to keep in touch with its customers and stakeholders with monthly and quarterly publications, such as the monthly *Tourism Update*, *Visitors Chronicle*, and presentations from our annual meeting and *Trends in Tourism* conference. Additionally, SCT reaches stakeholders through local media and press releases.

SCT has recently instituted a relationship with the Certified Tourism Ambassador (CTA) program, an international certification program designed "to train front-line employees and volunteers in the hospitality industry. The goal is to improve visitation by inspiring front-line hospitality employees and volunteers to work together to turn every visitor encounter into a positive experience (Sonoma County Tourism, 2013 A)." To date over 1000 Sonoma County tourism-related professionals have completed the certification.

Sonoma County Tourism: Organizational Mission, Vision, Values and Goals

The SCT website declares, "Sonoma County Tourism exists to market and sell Sonoma County as a desirable destination to visitors who are traveling for leisure or business. In other words, SCT's goal is to put more heads in lodging properties' beds (Sonoma County Tourism, 2014 C)." Their core values are "accountability, innovation, leadership, transparency, and diversity. These values drive our strategic planning, and affect decisions for sales, marketing, and operations (Sonoma County Tourism, 2014 A)."

The SCT *Annual Report 2013, 2014 Marketing Report* begins with this promise: "As professionals living and working in this region, the Sonoma County Tourism team is committed to moving Sonoma County forward and growing the economy through tourism. We are committed to these core values that drive our passion for this industry, our organization, and our community (Sonoma County Tourism, 2014 C):

Integrity: We accept only the highest ethical standards in all of our activities, including sales, marketing, public relations, and accountability.

Partnership: We are 'synergistic glue,' engaging our region in building relationships to further our mission and promote a stronger visitor industry.

Service: We commit to delighting our customers for going above and beyond their expectations for service.

Innovation: We are leaders in innovative programming, sales, marketing, and technology, leading the charge in positive destination marketing and economic growth.

Passion: We enthusiastically promote our destination and organization, inspiring community pride in our region's diverse assets."

To Tim Zahner, these terms take on more expanded definitions (Zahner, 2014).

Mission: Zahner repeatedly affirms that the mission, the purpose, of Sonoma County Tourism, is the promotion of Sonoma County as *the overnight* destination. He states emphatically that "the mission (of SCT) is really to promote Sonoma County as an *overnight* destination. Period."

Vision: Zahner begins by qualifying his answer with, "the vision of the Board, not directly this organization, is to raise the taxes collected, the county Transient Occupancy Tax, the 'TOT,' by 25% within five years (of 2007)."

However, to Zahner "the vision of the organization and the staff is to have a Destination Marketing Organization (DMO) that is one of the best in the industry with the straight goal of encouraging visitors to come here for overnight stays."

Goals and Values: Zahner expands upon the SCT website declaration by adding, "Our goals *are* accountability, innovation, leadership, transparency, and diversity."

Describing accountability, Zahner states, "A lot of DMOs have run afoul of their stakeholders and their funders when they aren't held accountable or take a keen look at ROI. We are."

Describing innovation, Zahner states that there are two areas SCT has been especially innovative (Zahner, 2014):

Always asking "What (from our customers' point of view, the potential travellers) can we do to always be 'top-of-mind' in the travel-making decision?"

The organization's funding models. "When we were founded we were one of the first Business Improvement Areas using the 'California Highways Code 36-500, et. seq.' We looked at how to fund an organization that wasn't reliant upon either the annual or bi-annual whims of city budgets. The Founders of this organization decided to find a way to find a dedicated and protected revenue stream, so they assessed a tax on themselves via a Business Improvement Area (BIA) assessment, a real innovation."

Describing leadership, Zahner states, "We want to be one of the best Destination Marketing Organizations (DMO) in the country. We want to compete not just with our natural competitors, Napa, Palm Springs, Santa Barbara, Monterey, with whom we compete for that overnight business, but we also want to on par with the large DMOs like San Francisco, LA, and Chicago. We ask, 'how can we do this together and what can we accomplish by using the different resources out there? (Zahner, 2014)'"

Describing transparency, Zahner states, "All of our meetings open to the public. We 'Brown Act,' which, in California, means open meetings. If you want to come to our Board Meetings, you can sit right next to me and make public comments, if you choose (Zahner, 2014)."

Describing diversity, Zahner states, "its easy to say diversity is simply saying you are going to target LGBT or multi-cultural segments. But diversity is, also, seeing Sonoma County as a destination of regional variety." Zahner emphasizes, "We take great pains to assure that everyone can see these different regions. This is a huge differentiator, especially when talking wine tourism. He offers as an example, "of course, we do have 400 wineries that are open to the public, but we also have the ocean. That makes us different! You can come here and go wine tasting then go out to Salmon Creek and walk along the coast; this, too, is part of our diversity. It's not just the core audience, it's the diversity of our destinations (Zahner, 2014)."

To facilitate this diversity, Zahner and his staff split the County into three regions (Zahner, 2014):

Valley and vineyards: Sonoma to Rohnert Park and heading northward, what Zahner considers the "main" wine region.

Rivers and Redwoods: "The Russian River, the Gualala River and the Petaluma River and, of course, the Redwoods."

Coasts and Sea Villages: The Pacific Ocean and San Pablo/SF Bay, an area Zahner emphasizes is a "great migration route for birds and birders, as well as fishermen."

Sonoma County Tourism: Organizational Promotion

Sonoma County Tourism is first and foremost a marketing organization. Just about every activity they perform is marketing based. Marketing is not simply advertising. According to the American Marketing Association, "Marketing is the activity, set of institutions, and processes for creating, communicating, delivering, and exchanging offerings that have value for customers, clients, partners, and society at large (American Marketing Association, 2014)." In other words, it is "the performance of a set of activities that seek to accomplish an organization's objectives by anticipating customer or client needs and directing a flow of need-satisfying goods and services from producer to customer (Perreault, 2010)" To Zahner, the product they sell is Sonoma County, the destination. He repeats, "the destination is the brand and this is what SCT sells (Zahner, 2014)." Their website declares, simply, "We market and sell Sonoma County (Sonoma County Tourism, 2014 C)."

There are two complementary facets to SCT's promotion. First, SCT must elicit the support of its primary customer, the tourism-based businesses in Sonoma County. They must make this community know that SCT is there to support and to promote them. Second, SCT must bring Sonoma County to the rest of the planet.

According to Zahner, to promote SCT to its business customer base, SCT employs a host of marketing tools, including (Zahner, 2014):

The SCT website. Zahner describes this as a full-service website for customers and partners detailing up-to-date information about SCT and the business community. Any Sonoma County tourism-related business can add content to website. SCT encourages businesses to "connect with us" on our "Partners page" at www.SonomaCounty.com/partners. On the Partner's Page the business is encouraged to advertise events, update listings, find leads, host journalists and trade, and participate in SCT activities (Sonoma County Tourism, 2014 D):

The mailing of the monthlies, *Tourism Update* and *Visitors Chronicle*.

The publishing presentations from their annual meeting and Trends in Tourism conference.

The use of press releases about the organization and the industry.

"Coffee Klatches." An informal meeting with industry professionals "over coffee" to explain, in brief to the community, what SCT is doing and has done to date.

The Partner Information Program (PIP). The PIP is essentially an invitation to five businesses at a time to come into the SCT office for a "speed dating" session. Upon completion, the business may introduce itself to the full Board and the community attending the meeting.

Informal Meetings by appointment.

Spontaneous "Walk-ins," wherein SCT walks into a community tourism-related business for an introduction to SCT.

The CTA program.

According to Zahner, to promote SCT to a worldwide customer base, including leisure travellers, tourism-related decision makers, and partners, SCT employs a host of marketing tools. Zahner explains, "the core is we go to people at some point in their decision-making process that Sonoma County is the 'correct answer' for their overnight visits, whether that visit is by a leisure traveller, or a meeting planner, or the tour operator." This process includes "everything" as simple as (Zahner, 2014):

Email campaigns.

Attending conferences and trade shows wherein SCT "shares the booths and marketing efforts of trade partners and alliances."

Making multiple visits to overseas tourism-related offices to "shake hands."

Participating with other tourism-focused groups, such as Brand USA (an internationally-focused organization), VisitCalifornia (a nationally-focused organization), regional and municipal Chambers of Commerce, and the marketing groups of individual cities and towns.

The placement of advertisements where SCT can maximize its exposure dollars: print, online, broadcast, and social media. Zahner emphasizes he is "always looking for ways to convince his customers that their wants are their needs and they need to come to Sonoma County to spend the night."

Sonoma County Tourism: Organizational Funding

SCT is not a membership, fee-based organization. It receives funding from two primary sources, an assessment on applicable lodging rooms within the Sonoma County Tourism Business Improvement Area (BIA) and a direct Sonoma County tax on accommodations at lodging and camping facilities in the unincorporated areas of the County. A third funding source is a "catch-all" pool of funds SCT entitles, "Other Income," such as the receipt of rents from the "Trio," more of an offset than income, Zahner explains (Zahner, 2014)."

The majority of SCT's funding comes from a two percent assessment on "applicable lodging rooms within the Sonoma County Tourism Business Improvement Area (BIA) (Zahner, 2014)." This assessment was initiated by the County in 2004 to promote tourism in Sonoma County by supporting organizations like SCT.

The assessment was created by County "Ordinance No. 5525" of November 2004, an ordinance of the Sonoma County Board of Supervisors, which effectively established, first, the Sonoma County Tourism Business Improvement Area (BIA) in "various cities of Sonoma County and in the unincorporated area of the Sonoma County," and, then, an assessment upon the earnings by any "lodging establishment (within the BIA) generating a total rent during the preceding fiscal year (July 1 to June 30) of greater than $350,000 (County of Sonoma, 2004)." Revenues from Assessments shall be used to conduct Marketing Activities designed to increase overnight visits to the Area. Revenues from Assessments may be used for programs, services, and activities outside the Area, if such programs, services, and activities are designed to promote and encourage overnight visits to the Area. Revenues from Assessments may also be used to pay or reimburse administrative costs incurred by the Contractor or County of Sonoma in connection with the creation of the Area and the Sonoma County Tourism Bureau, the transition of the current County-operated tourism marketing program to the Contractor, and the ongoing administrative costs associated with the Marketing Activities (County of Sonoma, 2004)"

Generally, sixty percent of SCT's revenue is generated by BIA assessment funds. In 2013, SCT collected $3,389,170 in BIA assessment funding, about 61% of their funding receipts (see Figure 11).

A second revenue source, representing about a third of SCT's annual revenue, is a nine percent "Transient Occupancy Tax," or "TOT." According to the County, "the Transient Occupancy Tax (Hotel, Motel, Campground or Bed Tax) is authorized under State Revenue and Taxation Code Section 7280, as an additional source of non-property tax revenue to local government. This tax is levied in Sonoma County at a rate of 9% for accommodations at lodging and camping facilities in the unincorporated areas of the County. TOT funds are discretionary, in that the Board of Supervisors may direct use of these funds for any legitimate county expense. The tax code does not require any specific use of the Transient Occupancy Tax (TOT) Funds. The Sonoma County Board of Supervisors has established a policy that the funds raised from this tax will be used, in part, to finance advertising and promotional activities in Sonoma County. Funds raised from this tax will be used, in part, to finance advertising and promotional activities in Sonoma County (County of Sonoma, 2014)." Zahner says, "the funds are collected by the County and, per our contract with the County, redistributed to us (Zahner, 2014)"

Generally, thirty-eight percent of SCT's revenue is generated by TOT taxes. In 2013, SCT collected $1,995,910 in TOT tax funding, about 36% of their funding receipts (see Figure 11).

The third revenue source, representing about three percent of SCT's annual revenue, is actually a collection from various revenue sources, including, but not limited to grants, awards, a percentage of membership receipts from the County Tourism Ambassador program, and interest on savings (Zahner, 2014). In 2013, SCT collected $163,526 in "Other Income" funding, about 3% of their funding receipts (see Figure 11). Again, claims Zahner, most is more of an offset than income (Zahner, 2014).

Zahner is proud that their funding model is innovative. The funding model, specifically crafted to not be membership-based, steers the organization away from the "admin problem of maintaining and finding new members due to continuous attrition and drop-off" and creates, in its place, a secure, perpetual funding-model not dependent upon membership. Instead, the model permits SCT to focus upon increasing "heads in beds." Zahner explains, "Though there is no *direct* return to us, there is still that two percent of their hotel stay revenue; we get two percent on all hotel stays within the BIAs. Thus, by increasing the hotels' gross, the two percent grows and all are happy (Zahner, 2014)."

The same is true for the TOT, of which SCT receives about 25% of the total tax received annually. Zahner further explains how this motivates his organization, "I can't create more hotel rooms or control the rates, but I *can* fill the vacancies. As a DMO, our job is to increase the occupancy (Zahner, 2014)."

Expenses are carefully monitored, measured and recorded by the Finance Department. From the website that department states, "the primary goal of the finance department is improving fiscal and administrative efficiency, accountability and transparency while enabling other departments to focus their efforts on the sales and marketing mission of SCT (Sonoma County Tourism, 2014 C)."

The expenses are bundled into broad categories associated with department of end use. The categories and their percentage of total budget are: "Leisure," at $2,872,084, representing 61% of the 2013 SCT program budget; "Meetings and Groups at $1,426,149, representing 30% of the 2013 SCT budget; and "Tour and Travel" at $422,982, representing 9% of the 2013 SCT budget (Sonoma County Tourism, 2014 C)

From the Annual Report for 2013 come the actual and budgeted revenue and expenses for 2013 1nd 2014 (Sonoma County Tourism, 2014 C):

Figures 11 and 12: The Sonoma County Tourism Revenue and Expenses, 2013 and 2014
Source: (Sonoma County Tourism, 2014 C)

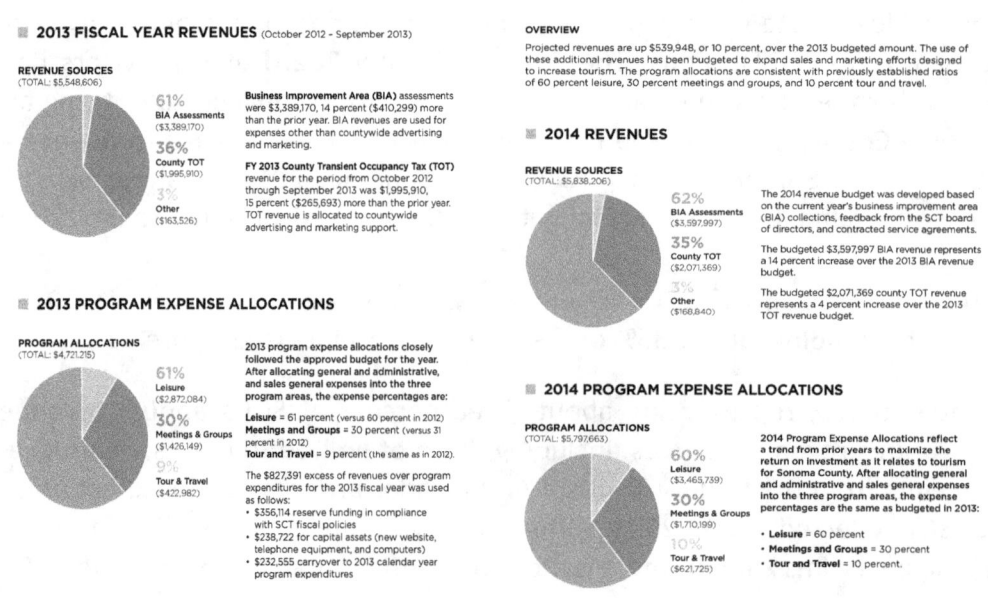

Sonoma County Tourism: Organizational Partnerships

Zahner quickly break his partnerships into four categories: the "Trio," marketing partnerships, strategic alliances, and other "allied organizations." In the world of marketing Sonoma County, however, the most notable and strategically advantageous partnership to SCT is the beneficially-crafted alliance between the three primary organizations, Sonoma County Tourism, Sonoma County Vintners, and Sonoma County Winegrowers. Zahner affectionately refers to this alliance as the "Trio" (Zahner, 2014)." To Zahner this relationship has permitted his organization, as well as the other two organizations, to expand and become successful far beyond what each could have accomplished independently.

The "Trio" partners and shares in many ways. They share a comfortably spacious, single level office suite tucked into cul-de-sac near Santa Rosa's Charles M. Schulz airport. They share a New York City PR agency. They share an in-house webmaster, a move that has permitted continuous, immediate, real-time shifts in their online marketing presence. They share a host of "assorted software," cutting well back on necessary expenditures. They share different marketing events, such as the very successful "Sonoma in the City," where tourism-related decision makers are brought into hear about the county, and they share "deskside visits," where the Trio huddles up against the desks of decision-makers to present the County, or something new about the County. This partnership, according to Zahner, has been the most transformational and effective bringing daily compounded leaps in ROI (Zahner, 2014).

A second level of partnership is "pay-to-play" marketing partnerships. In these partnerships, SCT joins an organization, via a paid membership, so as to participate in events or gain access to that organization's membership, relationships, and/or customer base.

A third level of partnership is Strategic Alliances. Zahner explains that these partnerships are not "pay-to-play." "We don't give them money, but we are allied organizations. Primarily we do research together (Zahner, 2014)." Examples are the regional and County parks, the Charles M. Schulz Airport, the Sonoma County government, and local chambers of commerce.

The fourth partnership grouping is what Zahner terms, "other allied organizations," organizations that perform the same, or similar, functions as SCT, but with a different geographic spread. Examples are Visit California, the self-described "official consumer web site of the State of California (Visit California, 2014 C)" and San Francisco Travel, an organization whose organizational goal is much like SCT's, "to enhance the local economy by marketing San Francisco and the Bay Area as the premier destination for conventions, meetings, events and leisure travel (San Francisco Travel, 2013)."

Tim Zahner: Best Practices, Advice and "Words of Wisdom"

Tim Zahner is truly a wealth of knowledge. Eight years as Director of Marketing has brought much understanding. To Tim, though the organization has experienced great success, keeping growth in check must remain a real focus: growth is, and continues to be, a great concern to him. Nevertheless, because of his success, when asked, Zahner is able to offer advice: if he were to advise another organization like SCT in another part of the country, what would he suggest they must do? Here is a synopsis of his "short list" of "Best Practices (Zahner, 2014):"

"Don't be married to your ideas. Let other people own the idea. As an example, when we were developing the new Sonoma Brand with Sonoma County Vintners and Sonoma County

Winegrowers four to five years ago. It could have been each organization saying this is who *we* are and your approach is bad. But we decided to own it together and not play that parochial, 'we.'"

"Proximity breeds friendships. Being 'co-located' is a huge assistance. When working with the Trio, we don't necessarily need to like each other; it's just that we live next to each other. It's the 'bumping into' and being able to ask, 'I've got a question about X.'"

"The fact that we convene quarterly the President's Council of the three 'Trio' Presidents, as well as all of the AVAs and Wine Road, to talk about issues that transcend our individual organizational barriers, is a huge advantage to us. We discuss not just winery-related or tourism-related issues: here we can bring into light and discuss issues facing all of us, such as water and the drought, etc."

"The sharing of resources is clearly a best-practice. We could not afford our national PR firm or our building space if we were not working together under one roof. The common sharing of employees, advisors, equipment and time together is a huge money saver."

"Realize who your customers are and what your customers want; then, give it to them! Remember that our brand is our destination! And remember that Sonoma County is really more fantasy than a reality (nobody really should eat 8000 calories of Prosciutto and Chevre and drink a gallon of wine and sleep in every day). That's 'Fantasy Sonoma County.' The reality is watching me at my house wrestle my kid out the door to school every day and watching my dog being a pain in the butt because he had been eating something nasty. We live quite ordinary lives here. So, we sell a fantasy. And, quite frankly, it's a very approachable fantasy. But that's the brand we sell."

"Give your customer what they want. When our customer comes out to Sonoma County, we need to discover what they want, then, give it to them. But do not try to convince them to buy something they don't want because they'll be pissed off when they come here expecting Orlando but do not get Orlando. Notice we never say, 'Go swimming at the beach.' We say, come 'explore our beaches.' We can fish, crab, stroll, but not swim. We use to say the come explore the 'rugged Sonoma coast.' Now we say come explore the 'scenic and majestic coast.' Its basic 'marketing-speak.' We are not Anaheim, we are not Santa Monica, we are not Hawaii. We are, however, wine and food and scenic beauty. Tell the truth. Mislead the customer about what to expect and they will not only never come back again, but they will assuredly tell Trip Advisor."

Tim Zahner: Challenges

Again, Tim Zahner is a wealth of knowledge. If Zahner were to advise another organization like SCT in another part of the country, what would he suggest they must strive to avoid? Here is a synopsis of his "short list" of "Challenges (Zahner, 2014):"

"I would advise a tourism organization to have a Board of Directors that provides clear direction on 'where to go,' especially when the Board is comprised of, for example, hotel General Managers who are use to being the 'Voice of God' on their own properties, but now find themselves just one member among equals. This group decision-making requires a different subset of skills than what parochially-minded GMs normally use. Thinking back to 'Marketing Federalism,' we must explain to our Board members that we all have 'confirmation bias' to overcome when working within a group of equals. Therefore, when meeting, we must take off the 'parochial regional hats' and put on our 'Sonoma County hat.'"

"Communication between departments is difficult because my team, I would argue, is very tech savvy because we live-or-die by technology and we must, therefore, stay up-to-date. Sometimes other staffers aren't as up-to-date, so when we adopt a new program that is technologically challenging, we will need to train the other staff members so as to help them into using successfully the new program."

"Organizational decision making is a huge issue. Here I am referring to how we are to make decisions in cases where we have not mapped out a response, a strategy. In our case, if you are 'lodging,' we really understand you. If you are a winery, we kind of understand you. If you are a restaurant, we kind of know how to deal with you. However, if you are something really brand new, at first, we were not so good in relaying back to you what we knew about you. A perfect example is answering how we are to treat a business not located in Sonoma County, like 'Red and White Fleet,' a Napa bus company, but using our roads and visiting our destinations. May we admit them into our fold? Can they access our bundle of value? Initially, we would do nothing. We had no answer, so we didn't answer. We had a real problem with figuring out new things and responding back. Hotels can't move, but a bus company? Now, we, as a staff, will adopt a recommendation and submit to the Board. Another example is how to deal with city of Sonoma and Healdsburg businesses that were non-BIA, non-lodging businesses yet wanted to work with us? Our initial policy (a bad policy, by the way) would be to exclude them. It began to breed resentment. It took us three years to realize that *we* visit Healdsburg and Sonoma with our own money on the weekends because we live right next door to them. So first, we looked at marketing 'opt-in program,' a hybrid of the BIA and a membership model, but this meant we would need to hire a membership manager with revenue and membership goals. This is clearly not what we want to include in our business model. So we made the right choice: we decided with our Board to include tourism-related, but non-lodging, businesses (like 'Zin Restaurant') in those cities. We do not want to compete with their Chambers, but *their* success is *our* success. But it took the Board and our staff undergoing a huge mind-shift to make the change. So, as a young organization, you must decide how to deal with things you do not know the answers to. Set procedures and timeframes on how to do so. This is classic 'managing expectations.'"

Choose really good coffee.

Tim Zahner: Sonoma County Tourism 2013 Successes and 2014 Plans

Tim Zahner points to the Annual Report when seeking to highlight the successes of 2013 and the plans for 2014. From the prologue (Sonoma County Tourism, 2014 C):

Because of SCT's successful programs, the tourism economy had a good year in 2013.

Occupancy at lodging properties grew by more than 9 percent, and lodging properties were able to raise rates, generating more revenue for businesses and local governments.

According to the Annual Tourism Survey of more than 300 tourism-related businesses in Sonoma County, 87 percent are "optimistic" or "somewhat optimistic" about their prospects for next year.

The Annual Report highlights these "Successes in 2013 (Sonoma County Tourism, 2014 C):"

Graduated more than 900 people in the Sonoma County Certified Tourism Ambassador program, 80 percent above the goal of 500 for the first year.

Launched a new website that saw a 90 percent increase in web visitation, with an incremental increase in destination spending of more than $10.6 million.

On the sales side, lead generation was up 6 percent with room nights booked up nine percent, which generated an economic impact of $5.1 million dollars. Weddings generated more than 177 leads with a nine percent increase in definite bookings.

Shared the Sonoma County Brand, an initiative with the Sonoma County Vintners and Sonoma County Winegrowers (known collectively with SCT as the Trio and will be referred to as such throughout this document) with other allied entities such as Visit Santa Rosa, Petaluma downtown Association and Visitors Center, Sebastopol Area Chamber of Commerce, and Sonoma County Harvest Fair.

Continued pursuing international markets, building relationships with tour operators and media in the U.K., Germany, Australia, New Zealand, Canada, Mexico, and Asia.

The Annual Report highlights these "major initiatives for SCT" in the coming year (Sonoma County Tourism, 2014 C):

Strong year-round advertising and marketing programs that promote Sonoma County as an overnight destination, coupled with seasonal campaigns regionally to bring in business during need periods.

A strong, viable brand message with each ad buy, sales connection, and marketing program, which will be enhanced by the conjunctive labeling law in the wine industry.

Increased representation in the Chicago, Northeast U.S., and Washington, D.C. meetings and group markets.

Growth in leads and visitation from international markets.

Continued support of the $54 million airport expansion and attraction of more air service connections to the Midwest and East Coast.

Continue offering the Sonoma County Certified Tourism Ambassador program.

Offer service-training opportunities to hospitality professionals throughout the destination, in order to make excellent service a hallmark of a visit to Sonoma County.

Tim Zahner: Dreams and the Future

Thinking of the future of the organization, Zahner offers short term, midterm, and long term goals and future plans. In other words, what would he really like to accomplish (Zahner, 2014):

Short term: "To increase the number of people who come here and the average 'daily rate' (the daily rate charged by hotels for a room). The Board wants this done. We cannot increase rates, but we can increase demand."

Midterm: "Our organization wants to show it is a legitimate organization now that we have reached our 'teenage years.' Yes, we will mature, but still stay lean. Other DMOs have crumpled because they have gotten 'fat.' One way we have managed to stay lean and, at the same time, not overtax our employees, is we lifted them to manager level so they could independently and more freely manage vendors. This way even tough they may not earn what they could selling 'widgets,' they remain extremely dedicated to Sonoma County and our organization. There is a greater sense of 'mission' here, of representing this place and all of these different businesses from small to large. It's a challenge, but the staff has stayed around. When I started there were only three of us in my department. Now, there is this thing called the internet. So, we have grown. But we want to grow in a way that is sustainable and does not take on new costs. We need and want a lot of money for programs, but as County tourism grows, so do we."

Longterm: "County lines are absolutely arbitrary. One funding traps is, 'Where you sleep matters.' Somewhere in the future we'll figure out how we manage our regions and experiences better. This requires 'seeing beyond your own hat.' This means some day taking in other areas: Napa, Marin. But how do we figure out a funding mechanism? How do we employ Marketing Federalism in a wider sense? If we really worked together hard we could take on Chile and France and Argentina. Wine does it, as with the Wine Institute. But we are not there yet. Maybe we need a Benevolent Dictator? Democracy is a messy thing. Visit Napa, but sleep in Sonoma? This is NOT the reality."

Sonoma County Winegrape Commission:

Sonoma County Winegrape Commission: An Introduction and a History

It was the rise to prominence of the California wine industry and, in particular, the rise to international recognition of the high quality of Sonoma and Napa County winegrapes, that "led the Grapegrowers of Sonoma County toward establishing an organization to represent them (Kruse, 2014)." According to Sonoma County Tourism, the "Sonoma County Winegrape Commission, dba Sonoma County Winegrowers (SCW), was established in 2006 as a marketing and educational organization, a state government agency, dedicated to the promotion and preservation of Sonoma County as one of the world's premier grape growing regions. With more than 1,800 growers, SCW's goal is to increase awareness and recognition of the quality and diversity of Sonoma County's grapes and wines through dynamic marketing and educational programs targeted to wine consumers around the world (Sonoma County Vintners, 2013 B)." Kruse adds, "We are a public entity under the oversight of California Department of Food and Agriculture (CDFA). We have a direct line from the USDA to CDFA to our organization doing business as the Sonoma County Winegrape Commission. In this way, we are unique, not like Sonoma County Tourism or Sonoma County Vintners. We are three unique business structures (Kruse, 2014). We operate as a marketing and educational California state government agency," Kruse adds.

According to Kruse, SCW started as a "grape growers association the 1980s. Similar to Sonoma County Vintners in that it was a membership-based organization that growers could opt into becoming a member. However, in 2004/5 there was talk among the growers to form a commission. In 2006, the growers voted to ask the state legislature to place a mandated assessment on their production on a per ton basis at .5% of the per/ton price receipt (Kruse, 2014)." This was the beginning of the Commission.

Kruse is quick to add, "This is not a sales tax. But the trigger is a sale. For example, if one grower is also a winery and all the grapes are used by that winery as an estate wine, there is no assessment because there was no sale. If no sale, there is no assessment. Additionally, the vineyard must grow and sell over twenty-five tons in all. Smaller vineyards are exempt. But the money goes in so we can help growers grow and market their grapes (Kruse, 2014).

Karissa Kruse, Sonoma County Winegrowers Commission President

Karissa Kruse came to the Sonoma County Winegrowers (SCW) as its Director of Marketing in September of 2012 and was named President for the organization when outgoing President, Nick Frey, retired on May 1, 2013 (Rebuild the United States, 2013). Born in Sioux Falls, South Dakota and growing up in Colorado Springs, Colorado, the last place Karissa believed she would wind up is the wine industry (Onit Consulting, 2014).

Kruse earned a BS in Economics and an MBA in Marketing from Wharton School of Business at University of Pennsylvania (Rebuild the United States, 2013). Following graduation, she worked in various capacities, primarily marketing, brand management, and business development, for several nationally know firms, such as General Mills, Universal Studios, Mattel, and Dairy Management (where she worked for seven years on behalf of dairy farmers nationally, she writes post-interview) (Rebuild the United States, 2013) and the Department of Defense (Sikara & Co., 2011). In 2007, while in Los Angeles, Karissa, with her business partner, winemaker Justin Harmon, founded Argot Wines (Sikara & Co., 2011). Today, she owns a twenty-five acre parcel in Bennett Valley, with five acres planted to grapes (Rebuild the United States, 2013) making her a winegrower in addition to working for winegrowers, she adds.

As Kruse tells it, coming on board at SCW as the Director of Marketing began with a discussion with Nick Frey. Together, they concluded that she would be the ideal successor when Frei left his post. The time spent as Marketing Director "was an opportunity to come in and get to know the role, the growers, the job, and a chance for them to meet me. It was a courtship, of sorts (Kruse, 2014)." However, Kruse is quick to point out that she "still went though a rigorous interview process: Board Interviews and meetings with growers (Kruse, 2014)." But in the end, she was chosen for the position; and she has not set still since. "Every day now my schedule gets shuffled. Not sure if I know yet all that I will be doing. This year, the drought. This afternoon I am on radio. I have a twenty-person board nominated and voted by growers representing the sixteen AVAs and the different areas of the county. I meet with them monthly every month for ten months of the year. During the harvest months, I meet with the executive committee (the chairs of our committees): the Marketing, Grower Programs, and Finance Committees. They are all advisors to me and I to them (Kruse, 2014)."

Additionally, Kruse is on the board of the Sonoma County Harvest Fair, Sonoma County Grape Growers Foundation, Sonoma County Tourism, Santa Rosa Chamber of Commerce, the Santa Rosa Junior College Viticulture Advisory Committee (Rebuild the United States, 2013) and a member of Leadership Santa Rosa Class 29.

Sonoma County Winegrape Commission: Organizational Structure

The Sonoma County Winegrape Commission (SCW) was established in 2006 as a marketing and educational organization dedicated to the promotion and preservation of Sonoma County as one of the world's premier grape growing regions. SCW, a state government agency, has oversight by California Food and Agriculture which supports producer regions (Kruse, 2014). Representing over 1800 grape growers, it is headed by ten Commissioners (and ten "Alternates") that form the Board of Directors. The Board, composed of a Chairman, a Vice-chairman and a Treasurer, hires the managing staff, led by Karissa Kruse, its President (Sonoma County Winegrowers, 2013 A). Kruse adds, "We are under the oversight of California Department of Food and Agriculture (CDFA). We are in District Three, which includes Sonoma County and approximately ten vineyards in Marin County, but we do business as Sonoma County Winegrowers. There is oversight by CDFA. They come to our board meetings. We post our public agendas on their website. They help audit our books, our financials. We 'live' under their 'umbrella.' (Kruse, 2014)."

Kruse exudes confidence and pride in her organization and her staff, stating, "My staff is the most amazing staff!" That staff is run by three other managers who are hired by the commission. Those positions are (Sonoma County Winegrowers, 2013 A):

Operations and Consumer Education Manager, Ginger Baker. According to Kruse, "She helps with office management and our sponsorship programs, a funding source for us. She collect the assessments and runs the new program, 'Ag Ed (Kruse, 2014).'"

Grower Programs Manager, Karen Thomas. Kruse adds, "She manages our over sixty educational programs. She has a committee that works with growers, vintners, and vineyard managers to define the hot issues so she can set the calendar for the year. She, also, puts that schedule online (Kruse, 2014)."

Marketing and Communications Manager, Sean Carroll. Kruse says, "He is my 'Right-hand Guy,' since I am the 'pseudo CMO,' since so much of what we do and what we spend is geared toward marketing. He works with media, with our PR agency, develops the 'creative,' writes our press releases… He is kind of a 'jack-of-all-marketing-and-communication' trades. He took my place. I once had that job (Kruse, 2014)."

In addition to the managers, others are part of the staff:

A part-time bookkeeper, who works as an independent contractor. Kruse adds, "She is helping us three days a week. She cuts checks, runs payroll. She attends our Finance and our Board Meetings. We get audited by CDFA and she keeps us on track. We report to the Board monthly, so we have a monthly Financial Board meeting just before that. CDFA is there each month. Our Fiscal Year runs July 1st to June 30th. Our annual audit is just after that. We have an independent auditor come in to check our books. Then, we give that to CDFA to validate. Additionally, we get audited on any grants we receive. We have a really clean shop, CDFA says. And this is due in large part to her (Kruse, 2014)."

A web developer, Jeff Herdell, who, though on the SCW payroll, is shared with the "Trio (Kruse, 2014)." He manages all of the three organizations' websites, web development, and SEO. He navigates all three organizations successfully, Kruse adds.

And the organization is seeking additional staff members: a Sustainability Manager to "help support our new initiative in sustainability" and a Marketing Coordinator who would "report directly to Sean to be an administrative assistant and to support our marketing initiatives (Kruse, 2014)."

Kruse adds that due to growth, "We have the funding to support them. This is attributable to the momentum we have in the 'Trio,' the new 'Branding,' and the sustainability initiatives. We have been able to leverage partnerships and obtain grant dollars (Sonoma County Winegrowers, 2013 A)."

Sonoma County Winegrape Commission: Organizational Stakeholders and Customers

According to Kruse, there are several categories of stakeholders and customers (Kruse, 2014):

Our grapegrowers: "First and foremost, they are our members."

Wineries.

Our tourism partners: "The 'Trio.'"

Our Sponsors: There are so many including vineyard management companies; vineyard supply companies; American Ag Credit; Western Weather, who provides weather updates and data from weather stations that are phenomenal; and other stakeholders, such as Pest Control Advisors who provides our PCA breakfast."

Our workers: "They are so skilled!"

The community: "The wine industry provides sixty percent of the county 'GMP' (Gross Metro Product), based on the new economic impact study in 2012. Everyone in the community is affected by what we are doing here. There is a $13.4 billion wine industry impact."

According to the SCW website, sponsors fall in to many categories who may sponsor at five different levels of annual sponsorship between $350 and $10,000. The categories are: "Agricultural Lenders, Compost and Soil Products, Crop Protection, Erosion and Sediment Control, Grapevine Nurseries, Irrigation Monitoring and Supplies, Laboratory Services, Membership Organizations, Tank, Pond, Well and Water Treatment, Pest Control, Professional Services, Real Estate Brokerages, Seed and Fertilizer Sales, Solar Electric and Heating, Transportation, Vineyard and Industrial Supply, Vineyard and Winery Equipment, Vineyard Management and Consulting, Wine and Grape Brokers, Wine Industry Director Buyer's Guide, and Wineries (Sonoma County Winegrape Commission, 2014 D)."

Sonoma County Winegrape Commission: Organizational Mission, Vision, Values and Goals

The Sonoma County Winegrowers declares in their "Value Statement," "Sonoma County Winegrowers are family farmers who work hard every day to produce high quality grapes that are the foundation for world class wines. Growers are dedicated to sustaining their land for future generations. They preserve the land where they live and work and the water and air that they share with neighbors. Growers actively support their communities and are proud to be a part of Sonoma County (Sonoma County Winegrowers, 2013 A)." Their website declares, "Part of the mission of the Sonoma County Wine Commission is education and sustainable agriculture (Sonoma County Winegrape Commission, 2014 E)."

SCW states on their website that their goal is world-wide recognition of Sonoma County's premium wines. "We know that on average, one out of 20 premium bottles of wine purchased by our core target is from Sonoma County. We also know that sales of Sonoma County wines increase as consumers understand more about this region. Our goal is to increase the number of Sonoma County wines purchased locally, nationally, and internationally. We will do that by educating consumers and trade about who we are and what we bring to the table – literally (We Are Sonoma County, 2013)."

Kruse is quite sure of her general Mission, Vision, Values and Goals, though these items blur somewhat in to more general declarations:

Kruse says her *primary* mission is to "help grape growers in Sonoma County have a place for their grapes (Kruse, 2014)." This includes the "bigger picture of promotion, marketing, and the and establishing of Sonoma County as a world-class wine region (Kruse, 2014)." In this effort, to support their grape growers, this work takes on a number of different forms. One primary focus of their work is the marketing and promotion of Sonoma County as a top-tier destination and wine-producing region, especially their work in conjunction with the "Trio." A second focus is to their grape grower in terms of "education and outreach (Kruse, 2014)."

Kruse is quite proud as she highlights grower education. "When I say 'education,' it's grower education. Helping them, we put on an average of fifty to sixty grower education programs a year and those topics include everything from water conservation and management on farms to workshops for their employees done in Spanish. We, also, talk about training and safety and pruning tips. We do programs, which I really think is great, called the 'Smart Marketer.' This year we are expanding to a Smart Grower Program. This is where we come in and really educate growers as to how they can be better business managers, business owners, and marketers of their own grapes and vineyards (Kruse, 2014)."

Additionally, SCW seeks to reach the community. "We realized we do a really good job of marketing to the consumer and these education programs for the growers, but there was a gap in the middle around how we communicate and outreach to our own community to help our community members and our neighbors understand a number of things (Kruse, 2014)." For Kruse, that community outreach has two components: 1) it seeks to inform the community about the historic tie of the region to agriculture and SCW's continuing effort to keep the land sustainable and environmentally secure and 2) it seeks to encourage local consumers to drink locally. "If you are living in the Wine Country, we hope that some of our biggest supporters are our local community and, if you live here, you choose to drink wine produced here from the grapes that are farmed here and grown here. We want them to bring their families and friends out to our wineries and vineyards to explore and experience what we think is one of the best things Sonoma County has to offer (Kruse, 2014)."

However, Kruse' biggest initiative is the commitment by the SCW and the greater wine industry in general to seek "100% sustainability" in Sonoma County's wine producing community in five years. "We are in our first 45 days of what is a very bold goal and commitment to sustainability on behalf of the wine industry in Sonoma County. Over the next five years, by 2019, SCW, in partnership with Sonoma County Vintners, the growers and wineries partnered here in Sonoma County, commit to being 100% sustainable (Kruse, 2014)." Wine Spectator, in May 2014, entitled their article highlighting this effort, "Can Sonoma Wine Go 100 Percent Sustainable (Sonoma County Winegrowers, 2013 A)?" They conclude in the subtitle of that article, after speaking with Kruse who responded, "We figured the way to get recognized was put a stake in the ground and say, 'Lets be leaders,' that it can be done (Nigro, 2014)." Recounting New Zealand's winegrowers seeking the same end "attained an astonishing high level of compliance, falling just shy of 100 percent in their target year of 2012 (Nigro, 2014)."

Sonoma County Winegrape Commission: Sustainability Initiative

The 100 percent sustainability project is an energetic and complex undertaking. It requires great planning and the full "buy-in" of the county's grape growers. But, according to Kruse, this is a vital and a very achievable goal. Kruse explains, "So what does sustainability mean? There are a couple of different ways to look at it. First to understand that it is a *simple* approach to the complex process of assessing one's vineyard toward really important results, like having a business that endures; having people that are well trained, safe and respected; and having land that continues to remain in agriculture. All of this is backed by a more *complex* process that includes our participating in certified sustainability programs that have been vetted by experts and industry stakeholders for a number of years (Kruse, 2014)." These programs include a partnership of the Code of Sustainability Winegrowing, a project formed by the California Sustainability Winegrowing Alliance (CSWA), the Wine Institute, and the California Association of Winegrowers. Other applicable programs include associations Fish-friendly Farming, among others. This is, according to Kruse, "a real comprehensive approach with over one hundred assessments that growers and wineries will look at to rate their operations (Kruse, 2014). The key is that to be 'Sonoma County Sustainable' one must participate in a 'sustainable program' that has certification," Kruse adds later.

To Kruse, "Sonoma County Sustainable" is a "three-pronged approach: a focus upon the environment, social responsibility and our people, and the viability of our business, a business that endures. We have a bold, five-year goal and a plan in place in terms of how we help the growers assess their vineyards (Kruse, 2014)." First, sustainability focuses upon the *environment*, especially in "water usage, energy efficiency, soil analyses, vineyard canopies, and erosion control (Kruse, 2014)." Second, it focuses upon a *social* element, including "worker training and safety, our role in communicating with our neighbors, our contributing to the community (Kruse, 2014)." Third, it focuses upon *economic* viability, what Kruse calls "the foundation of sustainability (Kruse, 2014)." "Grape growers are running a business people. It's their livelihood; it pays for their family needs, meals, college (Kruse, 2014). If your business isn't viable, it doesn't really matter what else you do," she adds.

Kruse is sensitive to complaints concerning "greenwashing," which is a deceptive marketing practice by which "green PR" or "green marketing" is used to promote a false perception that an organization's products or policies are environmentally friendly (Karliner, 2001). Defending SCW and its members, Kruse argues, "A lot of people talk about sustainability, but is that something you are talking about or are you actually doing it? For us in Sonoma County, the programs we are looking at using, 'Lodi Rules,' 'Fish-friendly Farming,' and the CSWA program, all have third-party verification in the program; therefore, so we have third-party audits. We can help the growers with the self-assessment where they assess over one hundred practices that they are doing in their operation. But, then, there is a neutral, third-party auditing to validate and offer improvements. We are going to be transparent about this by having someone else come in to validate that this is exactly what we are doing, that we are really 'walking the talk (Kruse, 2014).'"

To Kruse, the biggest "eye-opener" about the institution of the initiative was the fact that as the growers completed their self-assessments most realized that they were already practicing sustainability. "Maybe we don't document or track like that, but we are probably doing most of it. Our farms are multi-generational, first planted with Russian fur traders and Spanish missionaries, and are now 3rd, 4th, 5th generation. By default we are sustainable (Kruse, 2014)."

In the words of the SCW website, the reasoning behind the plan for all vineyards in five years to be sustainability is, "Sonoma County has a heritage of farm families preserving their land for future generations. It is part of the very fabric that defines the Sonoma County wine region and is delivered in every bottle of high quality wine that proudly carries the Sonoma County designation. Sonoma

County's wine industry has long been at the forefront of creating and utilizing sustainable practices in the vineyard, in the winery, and in running their businesses. This expertise has now evolved into Sonoma County winegrowers and winemakers partnering together to establish the nation's first 100% sustainable county which will benefit the environment while meeting the needs of consumers as well as increasing efficiencies, eliminating waste and saving money. In the near future, consumers around the world will be able to purchase any Sonoma County wine with confidence knowing that it is an environmentally-sustainable wine (Sonoma County Winegrape Commission, 2014 F)."

To implement the program, "We will utilize a three-phased program to be completed within the next five years. Starting in February 2014, the first phase of this effort will focus on helping winegrowers assess their sustainable vineyard practices through trainings and educational sessions focused on land use, water quality assessments, and carbon emissions. The goal is to assess 10,000 to 15,000 vineyard acres per year for the next four years until every acre of planted vines are under assessment for sustainability. As vineyard acres are assessed, the Sonoma County Winegrowers will work with vineyards to achieve certification. Once the winegrower program has kicked off, focus will be expanded to work with wineries and winemakers to roll out sustainability assessments and certification all with a goal of 100% sustainability for the wine industry in Sonoma County by 2019. The key of sustainability is continuous improvement. Once all of the county's vineyards and wineries are recognized as sustainable, improvement plans will be developed to provide access to new production models, techniques and approaches (Sonoma County Winegrape Commission, 2014 F)."

Sonoma County Winegrape Commission: Organizational Promotion and Partnerships

According to Kruse, SCW has several promotional strategies that act in concert with their partners (Kruse, 2014):

First, SCW "looks to leverage partnerships." She cites her relationship within the "Trio" as being the most advantageous and effective. This includes the common branding, the "We are Sonoma County" campaign, and the common website.

Second, the program Kruse entitles, "Sonoma in the City." The program, Kruse explains, is "where we build an event to bring winemakers, growers, and tourism folks to different cities. It's the bringing of Sonoma County on the road to other cities to provide our 'experience' of what you would get if you came here to Sonoma County. It targets trade, media, and consumers in their markets." This has been a very effective program for the organization.

Third, Kruse says, the relationship and *combined* effort of the "Trio," the growers, and their other 3rd-party partners help them together "build credibility and reach more efficiently target audiences" via shared promotional campaigns. "Most notably, just lately, we have been featured in *Food & Wine Magazine*, the *Wall Street Journal*, the *San Francisco Chronicle*, and *Wine Spectator*, among others." Therefore, it is important, she stresses "to have continued dialogue with our partners where we look to not only buy ads together, but, also, to work together to get added value, such as sponsorships for events or promotion for events. For example, we have our program, 'Sonoma in the City,' where we go to other cities and present Sonoma County to publications or other organizations. This week, in New York City, we are there for a big event. We will supplement our effort there by co-sponsoring *Food & Wine Magazine's* 'Best New Chefs' event Tuesday night, our own 'Sonoma in the City' event Wednesday, and, to help us build our relationship with *Food & Wine Magazine* on Thursday, we go into Food & Wine's offices to pour Sonoma County Wine and talk more about the region to their staff. So, it's really a nice continuity program to work with our partners in a unified effort."

Fourth, Kruse cites, again, "that pretty unique partnership with the Sonoma County AVA associations," now numbering sixteen. "As a 'Trio,' we have a quarterly Presidents Councilmeeting with the presidents of the three 'Trio' organizations, the leaders of the AVAs, and our Board Chairs to discuss countywide issues and opportunities to cross-promote and leverage each other for leads and dollars. This way we can share ideas and avoid mistakes by asking the AVAs to tell us what worked and didn't work. This assuredly, as an essential 'Best Practice,' helps us understand who has done what so we are not redundant. We get to know the 'points-of-contact,' so we are not all individually reaching out to the same person. We assign a 'relationship manager,' so we can build relationships, but not get in each other's way, especially when it comes to pitching a story to the media. We want to bring one, unified, 'big story.'"

Fifth, as an outreach, SCW employs a "Grant Program" wherein the organization provides matching funds to the AVAs to "help fund promotions that they do. We want to assist to make sure our AVAs are successful. We have 'seed money' for 'pilot programs' to leverage our dollars to help bring media to the area, to begin events, to update their websites, to create brochures, to create their maps. We will provide up to $20 thousand per AVA per year on a somewhat first-come, first-serve basis." Kruse explains that not every AVA can receive the matching funds every year, since SCW only has a revolving $150,000 to $200,000 set aside for the purpose. "The goal is to help the AVAs do those events and programs and get them off the ground and on their own. We want them to be able to afford to run these programs by themselves in three to five years with a positive ROI." In this way, the entire region will benefit from the efforts of a smaller organization. If, however, the program is not proving efficient or effective, SCW "help them find out why they haven't been able to do so. Maybe they have chosen a bad date or not providing enough consumer value or they are charging too much or not getting the right promotion."

The SCW website lists these additional promotional event-oriented activities so as to keep "our region top of mind for the important influencers covering harvest (Sonoma County Winegrowers, 2013 A)":

The Sonoma Wine Country Weekend, "the largest consumer wine event of the year, where Karissa acted as Master of Ceremonies at Crushpad's winemaking demonstration by providing the history of winegrowing in Sonoma County and answering consumer questions. We also created a popular display of the diverse soils found around Sonoma County, along with a variety of grape clusters and info describing each (Sonoma County Winegrowers, 2013 A)." Additionally, SCW "participated in a special VIP tour for media to preview the event's festivities, including Forbes.com, *LAX Magazine*, *Hollywood Reporter*, *Chicago Sun-Times*, *D Magazine*, *The Huffington Post*, and others (Kruse, 2014)."

The Sonoma County Harvest Fair where SCW "decorated our booth space with banners representing each AVA, along with the soil samples display." To SCW, "the best part was having some of our dedicated growers on hand to answer questions and interact with consumers (Sonoma County Winegrowers, 2013 B).

The first annual Fort Ross-Seaview Wine Festival where SCW spoke about "Sonoma County's vineyards and our 'Trio' partnership (Sonoma County Winegrowers, 2013 B) as part of a 'grant fund' Fort Ross-Seaview AVA received."

Grape Camp, where "we host twenty-five consumers and five journalists for a wine country 'boot camp for an unforgettable experience (Kruse, 2014)."

For their Growers, SCW provides the "Sonoma County Winegrape Commission's Grower Programs" which consists of "educational and informational meetings and events targeted to the farming and business needs of growers. The Grower Programs receive direction on topics and speakers from the Grower Programs Committee. The Committee is made up of growers, vineyard personnel, industry businesses and UCCE staff and is comprised of two task forces: Sustainable Practices and Business Programs. All meetings are held free of charge, except our '*Dollars & $ense Seminar*' and Annual '*Grower Barbecue* (Sonoma County Winegrowers, 2013 B).'" In the past fiscal year, SCW "organized fifty-eight grower meetings and events serving approximately 3,161 attendees. This is about 316 growers, vineyard employees, and industry members served by SCW each month during the 10-month meeting season (Sonoma County Winegrowers, 2013 B)." Those events include topics such as Sustainable Winegrowing, Integrated Pest Management (IPM), Organic Production, Employee Development, Recycling, Water Conservation, and Frost Protection, among others (Sonoma County Winegrowers, 2013 B).

Sonoma County Winegrape Commission: Organizational Funding

The Sonoma County Winegrape Commission (SCW) was established in 2006 as a marketing and educational organization, a state government agency, dedicated to the promotion and preservation of Sonoma County as one of the world's premier grape growing regions (Sonoma County Winegrape Commission, 2014 C). According to Kruse, "in 2004/5 there was talk among the growers to form a commission. In 2006, the growers voted to ask the state legislature to place a mandated assessment on their production on a per ton basis at .5% of the per/ton price receipt (Kruse, 2014)." Kruse is quick to add, "This is not a sales tax. But the trigger is a sale (Kruse, 2014)." This was the beginning of the Commission and, currently, the growers vote every five years to keep the Commission.

According to Kruse, funding for the Commission comes from three primary sources (Kruse, 2014):

First, funding comes from the assessment. The assessment provides the bulk of there funding at "about $1.2 million a year." Kruse explains, "The assessment is collected through the wineries in their contract with the Grapegrowers deducting the assessment from their payment to the grape growers. We work with the wineries to do the collection. This is clearly a trust relationship. Even though all purchases are weight-tagged, much of the grape contracting is still is done with a handshake." Kruse praises the "old school" nature of this collection. "Grower-winery relationships are amicable, a collaboration, a true relationship as they work together to promote SC." The money goes in so as to help growers grow and market their grapes. The commission is dependent upon the yield of the year. 2012 and 2013 were two banner years: we had extra money in our assessments. Kruse adds, "We are a marketing and educational state government agency under the oversight of California Department of Food and Agriculture (CDFA). We are in District Three, which includes all of Sonoma County and approximately ten vineyards in Marin County, but we do business as Sonoma County Winegrowers. There is oversight by CDFA. They come to our board meetings. We post our public agendas on their website. They help audit our books, our financials. We 'live' under their 'umbrella.' Grape assessments are triggered by a sale. For example, if one grower is also a winery and all the grapes are used by that winery as an estate wine, there is no assessment because there was no sale. If no sale, there is no assessment. Additionally, vineyards must grow and sell over twenty-five tons in all. Smaller vineyards are exempt. The money goes in so we can help growers grow and market their grapes."

Second, funding comes from grants. This money is especially important in low production years, like 2010 and 2011, since the assessment money is based on sales of grape production. This helps the organization bridge any shortfall and do additive marketing activities. The drought this year is a cause for concern. Kruse is anticipating a lower yield this harvest. "We are already looking forward to getting grants so we can bridge the drought for our programs and our employees, if things continue as they are," she says and staff our programs. It will be a low-tonnage year. We are very fiscally-responsible."

In 2012, SCW received a CFDA "Specialty Crop Block Grant," a two-year grant of federally-supplied funds designated for each state to use toward the "support" of agriculture, including marketing. SCW is in their second year of receiving these funds and just reapplied for a renewal of this grant.

Third, funding comes from sponsors. SCW has five levels of sponsorship, ranging from $10,000 a year to $350 a year. The website lists as the purpose and advantages of the sponsorship program, "As we promote Sonoma County both locally and across the country, we value the importance of brand recognition for Commission Sponsors and their annual budget considerations. There are many ways to participate and gain exposure for your brand and organization. Participating in our tradeshows gives you the opportunity to meet new contacts from your target audience or to get back in touch with existing customers and business contacts. We also provide opportunities for website spotlights, email and print advertisements and we are implementing a plan to increase search engine optimization on our Sponsor webpage (Sonoma County Winegrape Commission, 2014 G)." This includes, as well, other sponsorship opportunities supporting individual events, such as the "Weather Network Sponsorship," "Sonoma County Pruning Championship Sponsorship," and the second annual "Holiday Harvest Celebration."

Karissa Kruse: Best Practices, Advice and "Words of Wisdom"

Karissa Kruse is in continuous motion working as an advocate for Sonoma County grapes, as well as for Sonoma County. Like Zahner, she is a wealth of knowledge. Under her guidance the organization has grown and is scheduled for much more growth. Keeping a reign on that growth, keeping it in focus and in check, so as to manage that growth, is always a concern. Nevertheless, when asked, Kruse is able to offer advice: If she were to advise another organization like SCW in another part of the country, what would she suggest they must do? Here is a synopsis of her "short list" of "Best Practices (Kruse, 2014):"

"Figure out how *everyone* in the 'relationship' can get value. Within the 'Trio,' we had first to lay out 'how do we *all* get value from this relationship?' For grape growers, simply, by an increase in grape prices and margins: they need to be able to sell their grapes. Farming costs increase, but they need to see an increase in profit or they cannot stay in business and maintain a livelihood.

Wineries need to create more value for their wine to get greater margins and profits by getting a higher price from the consumer. For tourism, its 'heads in beds,' overnight stays. Those are the fundamental ways each organization has to build value for our stakeholders. As we looked at the model, we realized together that the more people that come to Sonoma County to experience Sonoma County, the more loyalty is formed to Sonoma County as a *whole* as well as to specific wineries. We know one of the top reasons tourists come here is for wine and, because of the wine, we can get people here to explore the beauty, the actual tasting, the restaurants, the chefs, etc. Over time (and our growers had to take the greatest 'leap of faith' in the partnership) that extra value delivered because consumers, appreciating Sonoma County wine, would choose to pay for it via loyalty; this would result in our grape growers always having a place to sell their grapes, always having an increase in price and *value* of their grapes. My advice is if you choose a partnership like ours, you need to lay this out and articulate to the Board and to stakeholders that this approach makes sense. Figure ahead of time, 'where does everyone sit in the value chain and how do you provide benefit back?'"

"Always seek to build relationships. The leaders of the 'Trio' get together at bi-monthly lunches to talk 'staff,' office space, key promotions, to make sure we are still aligned. Build a 'culture of collaboration.'"

"Know where your areas of expertise are. Our growers may be good at soils and farming, but they may not be the best speakers. They are a humble group who wants to stay on their farms and get the work done. Winemakers are much more public figures, as well people involved with tourism. So, how you leverage your stakeholders in how they participate in what you do is important. Even within your staff expertise, skills, etc. needs to be leveraged efficiently."

"Proximity is so important. The sharing of office space, for us, has been instrumental. It 'shortens' decision-making. It permits the sharing of staff and equipment, especially, for us, our web developer. It allows 'office conversations' that encourages a relationship among all of the staff. For example the Wall Street Journal promo that requires a 'sign-off' from all three organizations (because all are funding it)… we all have ads in it, we all developed the story for it. If we were in three different offices, this would be very difficult. Instead, we can 'pop in and out' of each other's offices to get that approval. The leaders are all three organizations are together so we can to align the 'course strategy' for the 'Trio.'"

"Having a single 'Brand.' Being assured that everyone is behind what it (the brand) really stands for allows us to have one voice in the community and in the marketplace."

"Populate each other's Boards. In this way you have an 'official' voice."

"Leverage each other's dollars. Work toward having a meaningful percentage split of 'things' as different opportunities come up, 'things' none of us could do alone."

Karissa Kruse: Challenges

Again, Karissa Kruse is a wealth of knowledge. The momentum of growth is a challenge. Therefore, given that growth, if Kruse were to advise another organization like SCW in another part of the country, what would he suggest they must strive to avoid? Here is a synopsis of her "short list" of "Challenges (Kruse, 2014):"

"Having multiple Boards and reporting structures is difficult. We have growers who are competitive, yet who are pretty aligned when it comes to how they navigate certain agriculture issues in Sonoma County. Our wineries are competitive in the marketplace, but find that common ground in how they make decisions together. Tourism has so many different businesses, from hotels to ziplines, so different Boards, different levels of engagement, different levels of alignment, can be challenging in terms of what their priorities are. That's why having 'Best Practices' discussed during the Joint Executive Committee meeting each year is really critical."

"Having different funding sources and different funding accountabilities. Ours is an assessment, so if you are a Sonoma County grower you're 'in.' Sonoma County Vintners is a membership, so they don't necessarily represent all vintners. Demonstrating value is always a challenge."

"Having, from our momentum and our great partnership, so many 'balls in the air' and still execute flawlessly can be a challenge and its up to us to continue to take up that challenge to take advantage of that 'snowball effect' of our branding and our messaging and our partnering. We don't want to lose that success, so we need to account for those long hours and juggling and a lot of strategic sweat equity. We need to know how to best leverage our resources."

"Accountability. We have accountability back to our growers. Sonoma County Tourism is responsible to the County for approval of their annual business plan by Sonoma County Supervisors. Sonoma County Vintners is driving membership trying to provide real value back to their members, but SCV must balance the 'contending' wineries' overlapping interests. We all must make sure we balance our representation of our stakeholders as well as the Sonoma County brand. That is a lot to manage and we each have small staffs. But we must always consider 'how to we give back to our communities, our partners?' Its never unique, it is just an added layer when you really think about trying to manage the values, priorities, needs, and resources of the three organizations trying to do a lot of joint programs. We must be accountable."

"I was not there, but trying to establish and get 'buy-in' to the Sonoma County Brand was a challenge, especially in determining what it meant in a way that was meaningful for all of the organizations. My advise to a new organization is to consider, before you go forward or public with your new brand with other organizations in a partnership, spend the time to align what the benefit and value to your organizations is so you can communicate why it makes sense to partner together. Pick those couple of 'things,' such as, 'how are you going to be meaningful with that 'one voice?' 'What does that 'one voice' stand for?' 'What is that brand message, the brand promise and equity?' Take the time to really ensure that the organizations, the partners, and associations that are joining are in alignment so that does not become the point of contention. Consider, then be sure that your goals, your strategic direction, are headed in the same direction so you can really spend time prioritizing it and maximizing both dollars and efficiencies."

Karissa Kruse: SCW 2013 Successes and 2014 Plans

Kruse lists in the Fall 2013 Vine Times, the SCW's quarterly newsletter, these objectives as important concerns for the future (Sonoma County Winegrowers, 2013 B):

Increasing the equity for the Sonoma County Brand.

Increasing the real and perceived value and demand of Sonoma County winegrapes.
Assuring economic sustainability of Sonoma County wine grape growing for the future.

Educating the public on the role of grape growing in Sonoma County.

The evolution of the sustainability effort for both vineyards and wineries in Sonoma County.

The SCW Vine Times Newsletter lists some of the additional successes of 2013 and the plans for 2014 not mentioned within this Case Study (Sonoma County Winegrowers, 2013 B):

The exceptional vintage for 2013 was a cause for celebration, though the drought casts a concern for the present harvest. Kruse's "President's Report" reads, "2013 delivered another exceptional harvest in Sonoma and Marin Counties. After the bounty of 2012, many were skeptical Mother Nature would not bestow kindness two years in a row. However, 2013 is shaping up to be an outstanding vintage in both quantity and quality."

The continued relationship with the "Trio" and the continuing success of the "We are Sonoma County" campaign and brand. Kruse reports, "Coming off of the new Sonoma County brand launch in August of 2012, this past year has been focused on building awareness of Sonoma County through national platforms and partnerships with *Food & Wine*, *Wall Street Journal* and *Wine Spectator*. Regionally, we hosted Sonoma in the City events in both Dallas and San Francisco and supported another wonderful 'Grape Camp' experience for 26 campers and four media representatives. We are just beginning to see the power of the partnership with SCV and SCT. Over the next five years, we will build on the momentum of promoting Sonoma County through more partnerships, new pilot programs, and further branding integration with the AVAs."

Holding firm to the direction provided by the "Strategic Plan" developed in 2009 to discuss "the direction for the Commission and District 3 grape growers for the next ten years. As a result, the focus of our discussion shifted to how we evolve the approach and execution while maintaining the strategy."

Karissa Kruse: Dreams and the Future

Thinking of the future of the organization, Kruse has but two additional dreams she wishes to share (Kruse, 2014):

"We want to continue the momentum. We just made the sustainability announcement. My wish is that in five years consumers have confidence that if they buy a wine from Sonoma County that it has been grown and made sustainably. I think this is going to take the effort of all of the organizations, the AVAs, in Sonoma County coming together with support from the community, support from our leaders, to make that happen."

"My personal vision is that Sonoma County continues to be seen as a place to come and explore; that it is about the people here: our growers, our winemakers, our hotel managers and staffs, who are all trying to create a great experience and who, also, live here, they are 'walking the talk.' This is their own community. They feel a special bond and an emotional connection to this place. I want the consumer to feel this as well."

Sonoma County Vintners:

Sonoma County Vintners: An Introduction and a History

Sonoma County Vintners is the oldest of the three agencies within the "Trio," founded in 1944. Their self-description within their website reads, "SCV is the leading voice of Sonoma County wine, dedicated to raising awareness and building understanding of Sonoma County as one of the world's premier wine regions, noted for its heritage of artisan winemaking, distinct growing regions, and extraordinary quality. Founded in 1944, SCV represents more than 250 wineries and affiliates of all sizes throughout the county (Sonoma County Vintners, 2013 B)." "Through member collaboration, we develop strategic partnerships and create promotional programs to enhance the reputation of Sonoma County and its wines worldwide. In 1989, we created the Sonoma County Vintners Foundation to conduct and support wine industry education and non-profit organizations providing services within Sonoma County (Sonoma County Vintners, 2013 C)."

Sara Cummings, the organization's Director of Communications, continues the narrative, "I believe it was found in 1944 by a group of ten vintners who saw the value in promoting the region. The group would go on national tours and have wine events here, but it wasn't necessarily as strategic as it is now. In the last ten years, with the arrival of Honore Comfort as Executive Director and the Board seeing a need for a new strategic vision, the Board realized we needed to jump into the next chapter of regional wine marketing organizational work. Honore joined in 2006 and we really made a move from being a trade organization that did rather typical and traditional trade organizational activities to a marketing organization where marketing really became 'Job One,' elevating our perception, appreciation and understanding through marketing (Cummings, 2014)."

SCV, unlike the other two "Trio" organizations, is a *membership-funded*, 501(c)(6) non-profit, an "Education Organization." Therefore, unlike the other two Trio organizations, their revenue is dependent upon a consistent dues-paying membership. Cummings quickly adds, that as a 501(c)(6), SCV "cannot get involved in governmental affairs (Cummings, 2014)." The IRS defines "a private, non-profit 501(c)(6) organization" as "an organization whose purpose is to engage in a regular business of a kind ordinarily carried on for profit, even though the business is conducted on a cooperative basis or produces only sufficient income to be self-sustaining. Its activities are directed to the improvement of business conditions of one or more lines of business rather than the performance of particular services for individual persons… which are not organized for profit and no part of the net earnings of which inures to the benefit of any private shareholder or individual (Reilly, 2003)."

Sara Cummings, Director of Communications

Sara Cummings has been with Sonoma County Vintners for five years. Her current position is the officially the "Director of Communications," and, as such, is thrilled to be a part of the organization. According to Cummings, her primary obligation is to "work on all levels of communication, from member programs to the website to press releases to strategic messaging (Cummings, 2014)." Also, as a singular additional responsibility, Cummings "oversees the PR as the 'PR Director' of the 'Sonoma Wine Country Weekend (Cummings, 2014),'" an annual fundraising event co-sponsored with the Sonoma Valley Vintners and Growers Association. SCV markets the event as, "Sonoma County's signature, and largest, charity event, bringing together over 200 of Sonoma's top winemakers and growers, along with a collection of the area's best chefs. Jointly produced by the Sonoma County Vintners and the Sonoma Valley Vintners & Growers Foundation, all proceeds benefit local charities (Sonoma County Vintners, 2013 B)."

Just prior to coming to SCV, Cummings was a local residential real estate agent, but worked in wine industry public relations for fourteen years before that.

Honore Comfort, Executive Director

Honore Comfort came to came to the Sonoma County Vintners as its Executive Director in 2006 (Cummings, 2014). According to Sara Cummings, this was a decisive point in the history of SCV, the point at which the organization moved from being "a trade organization that did rather typical and traditional trade organizational activities to a marketing organization (Cummings, 2014)." Prior to her position with SCV, Comfort was a "Senior Brand Manager" with Foster's Wine Estates, a subsidiary of the Australian wine and spirits giant, a "Senior Brand Manager" with Southcorp Wines, another very large Australian wine brand firm, and the "Director of Print Media" for Macy's West, a division of the famous New York department store (Honore Comfort, 2014).

Sonoma County Vintners: Organizational Structure

Sonoma County Vintners is a membership-funded 501(c)(6) non-profit marketing and educational organization. Representing over 250 wineries in Sonoma County, the organization is overseen by a "fourteen-member, 'managing' Board of Directors elected to two-year terms comprised of 12 vintners seats and two at-large community seats (Cummings, 2014)," according to Cummings. "Our goal is to have a cross-section of small, medium and large wineries with company wineries and family-owned wineries (Cummings, 2014)." The Board members' list reads like a "Who's who" in Sonoma County wine, including Matt Gallo of E&J Gallo, Jeff Bundschu of Gundlach-Bundschu, Dan Kosta of Kosta Browne, and Joel Peterson of Ravenswood, to name a few (Sonoma County Vintners, 2014 A).

The Board hired the Executive Director, Honore Comfort, in 2006, who, in turn, hired her six-person staff, four of whom hold "directors" titles: the Directors of Membership and Partnership Marketing, Communications, Marketing, and Events and Operations (Sonoma County Vintners, 2014 A).

The Directors are:

Kelley Perez, Director of Membership and Partnership Marketing.

Sara Cummings, Director of Communications.

Bryan Carr, Director of Marketing.

Dana Macaulay, Director of Events and Operations.

Membership is dues-base and based upon a winery's annual case production: under 6,000 cases pays a flat fee of $1,000 per year; over 6,001 cases pay $1,000 plus 10¢ per case over 6,001 cases per year with a cap at $10,000 (Sonoma County Vintners, 2013 C).

Sonoma County Vintners: Organizational Stakeholders and Customers

According to Cummings, there are several categories of customers and stakeholders (Cummings, 2014):

Customers:

Our members: "Happiness is 'Job One.' We want to deliver value to them."

Stakeholders:

Our wineries.

Our grape growers.

"Anyone interested in the value and perception of Sonoma County wine."

The Sonoma County Board of Supervisors: "Especially with TOT funding, keeping them in the loop of what is going on is important."

Media.

High-level consumers.

Influencers (gatekeepers) around the world: "These are important restaurants, high-level sommeliers and beverage directors, buyers for retail (for example Whole Foods and BevMo) and people who control decisions on a lot of wine that would be 'dealing' at the price points our wines are. We do a couple programs that target them specifically every year."

Trade Media.

Wine Country Weekend: "This is our huge Labor Day Weekend event with the Sonoma Valley Vintners and Growers Alliance and all Sonoma County Valley wineries."

Sonoma County Vintners: Organizational Mission, Vision, Values and Goals

Sonoma County Vintners declares in their "Mission Statement" that their purpose is to "Establish Sonoma County as the leading winegrowing region recognized globally for superior wine quality, varietal diversity, unparalleled scenic beauty, and culinary excellence (Sonoma County Vintners, 2013 C)."

The SCV website, in declaring the value in winery membership, claims, "Sonoma County Vintners is the leading voice of Sonoma County Wine, dedicated to increasing awareness and improving the quality image of our wines to consumers, media and trade - locally and globally (Sonoma County Vintners, 2014 B)" by:

Providing member services that define the standard for the California wine industry.

Establishing new standards for collaboration with other Sonoma County partners.

Pioneering new strategies and techniques for marketing our wines and wineries to the world.

Being the source for news and access to the Sonoma County wine industry.

Creating events and marketing programs that educate and entertain while conveying the outstanding quality of the world-class wines produced in Sonoma County.

SCV continues, "Whether your winery is big or small, well-known or just starting out, you are a part of the Sonoma County wine community. SCV enables established brands to help support the region they're a part of, new brands to gain a foothold, and everyone in between to have a voice in this wine region. No matter what your winery size, SCV membership is a great value - by leveraging the resources of our organization, your membership dues pay for themselves many times over (Sonoma County Vintners, 2014 B)."

Cummings is quite sure of her general Mission, but this merges within the vision, values and goals (Cummings, 2014):

Cummings states as her mission, "We are the 'brand champion' for Sonoma County as a wine region, locally, nationally, and globally. Our job is to educate influencers, decision-makers, media, and top-level trade to help them better understand and appreciate the complexities and the quality of our region."

Cummings says the long-term goal of SCV is "to increase the value of our wines and grapes from this region. One out of every twenty bottles over $15 sold is from Sonoma County. We want to increase that to two in 20. This is a five to ten percent increase in wine sales over the next five years. We are in 'Year Two'. With our brand launch late in 2012 our goal was articulated this publically."

Cummings, too, is proud of the "Trio's" new branding campaign and the logo "stamp." She says, "We began with the new 'stamp' with the winegrowers because we work particularly well together with them. Then, 'Tourism' liked it so much (though it was, at first, a dream that they would adopt it, as well), they totally embraced it with us. Therefore, our co-branding got further faster than we ever dreamed in terms of the adoption of the brand mark. It's our "company logo' and our 'advertising mark,' but it's mean to be shared."

Sonoma County Vintners: Organizational Promotion

Sonoma County Vintners has several promotional strategies that fall into two broad categories. First, SCV seeks to reach Sonoma County wineries to alert them to the organization's existence and to its benefits of membership. Second, SCV seeks to promote Sonoma County Wines to the national and global wine markets.

To reach Sonoma County wineries about SCV, Cummings lists (Cummings, 2014):

First, Cummings explains, "We don't advertise, per se: it word-of-mouth, some email, and a lot of personal follow-up. We have a Director of Membership who works on outreach. She keeps lists of wineries and folks that say they might be interested. Some call in because they have heard of us. But we are constantly out and about working on it." She explains that their continuous struggle is simply due to having to "compete" with so many contending dues-based organization, such as the individual AVA groups and "multi-regional organizations" like "Wine Roads," "Family Winemakers of California," or "ZAP," the "Zinfandel Advocates and Producers." With so many choices, Cummings explains, a winery "has to decide who's going to deliver 'bang for the buck,' which organizations are important. We have a great reputation for delivering really good work, they just have to choose." However, she is careful to highlight, "Even if they don't join, they benefit. Our 'rising tide will raise all the boats.' Some get that and value that and want to pay their fair share, but some can't afford it, think its too expensive, have other priorities, or they do a mix by alternating. Many market directly and some small wineries have no interest in other markets. But, we are like NPR: people listen, but don't join, yet still benefit."

Second, "We invite all interested wineries to our annual meeting as an outreach to current and potential members in January so they can see what we are doing and meet some of our people."

To promote Sonoma County wines, Cummings lists (Cummings, 2014):

International travel: "We do some international travel that is prioritized each year by the Board's interest. Canada is very important. So are Europe, Hong Kong, and Asia. Two years ago, for the first time, and this year, Honore and a small team of vintners will go to 'Expo Hong Kong' in June, as well as an additional ancillary tour. It includes seminars, tastings, and presentations of our topography, our fog patterns, our complicated soil, where we are, how big we are, climate and weather, why we can grow so many kinds of grapes so well. It starts with basic education and, then, of course, tasting. We do several a year reimbursed by MAP funds."

National events: "This year we are going to Southern California and New York City. We do so to touch trade and consumers with educational events and tastings with a number of our members travelling with us."

Tastings and presentations at high-level trade events.

The "Sonoma Summit:" "Every fall for three days in November we bring 35 top sommeliers, wine buyers, and decision-maker/gatekeepers here to several regions in Sonoma County for three days to taste almost 100 wines. They can see the topography and our different AVAs. They can go to the vineyards. They can have educationally-designed tastings with our varietals. Then, they will know our areas, our wines, and become ambassadors for Sonoma County wine. This is a touch-point!"

"The "Trio:" "Nick Frey (of Sonoma County Winegrowers) and Honore Comfort realized the value of working together was super-powerful: as wine perception goes up, grape production goes up. When 'wine people' come here to appreciate our wines, they stay in our hotels, so 'Tourism' cares. We are all in this together. A lot of regions don't work that way. Political boundaries, egos, whatever - they don't see the synergy of it, so it puts us at an advantage."

Visa Signature: "We work with Visa with special pricing and winemaker dinners around the country, about twenty-five of those a year, two a month. The funding is shared with Visa. We line up the wineries and get the logistics down. We are the 'conduit' to the 'stable' of wineries. This is another unique opportunity for the individual wineries."

Print advertising in "food and wine" magazines.

Online promotion: "Google ad placement to drive traffic."

The SCV website and social media.

Consumer events: "Sonoma Wine Country Weekend" and "Sonoma in the City."

Emailings.

Cummings makes quite clear, however, SCV does not promote individual wineries or labels. "Our job is to promote Sonoma County as a region and command a higher 'ding' and a larger percentage of a wine-buyer's pocketbook because we are so unique. We do this by convincing the wine buyer that this is a wine region of note, not just any wine region, so they are willing, over time, to buy more at a higher price. It is the winemaker's job to expose to the consumer to individual wines. On the web a consumer is coming into our site can first see the collective and, then, see the individual wineries. In this way, we all 'lift the whole boat (Cummings, 2014).'"

Sonoma County Vintners: Organizational Funding

Sonoma County Vintners is a membership-funded organization, from which the bulk of annual revenue is derived. Membership is dues-base, with currently "about 220 wineries and twenty-five to thirty 'affiliate members,' who are primarily industry 'folks,' such as barrel companies, banks (Cummings, 2014)," Cummings says. The dues are based upon a winery's annual case production: a winery producing under 6,000 cases a year pays a flat fee of $1,000 per year while larger wineries (over 6,000 cases a year) pay $1,000 plus 10¢ per case over 6,000 cases per year (with a cap at $10,000) (Sonoma County Vintners, 2014 C). "We are 100% member-driven. Every winery in Sonoma County has the option to pay dues and be active in our events and activities. Our goal is to have a cross-section of small, medium and large wineries with company wineries and family-owned wineries. The key to membership eligibility is not that they be here in Sonoma County, but that they produce Sonoma County wine (Cummings, 2014)."

A second source of funding, though smaller, is Sonoma County's Transient Occupancy Tax. Cummings says, "Our funding is supplemented through some TOT tax funds through the County, the same pool of funding supporting Sonoma County Tourism, but a smaller piece (Cummings, 2014)."

A third source of funding is grant monies, including federal "agricultural" grants, specifically "Value-Added Producer Grants" (VAPG) through the USDA. These are granted to SCV because the organization is "considered an agricultural marketing organization (Cummings, 2014)" by the federal government.

A fourth source of revenue is a reimbursement for "our international work through MAP funds (specifically-allocated, marketing-oriented funds) through the California Wine Institute, similar to what Sonoma County Tourism might get through VisitCalifonia (Cummings, 2014)."

Additionally, SCV partners with the "Trio" to promote "Sonoma County brands throughout the year to key media, trade and consumers (Sonoma County Vintners, 2014 C)." SCV requires wineries, therefore, to donate wine toward that effort. Smaller wineries are asked to donate six bottles a year and larger wineries, a case a year. Cummings adds, "However, some Sonoma County wineries produce wines from other regions fruit. They can't use those wines at our events. Event wines must be Sonoma County wines (Cummings, 2014)."

Sonoma County Vintners: Organizational Partnerships

According to the SCV website, the organization has several partner groupings. "Sonoma County Vintners works closely with several Sonoma wine, grape and tourism organizations to achieve our shared goals of increasing awareness of Sonoma County wines and encouraging travel here to experience Sonoma County firsthand. We are pleased to work with these wine and tourism industry partners (Sonoma County Vintners, 2013 D)." These include (Sonoma County Vintners, 2013 E):

The "Trio," the partnership with Sonoma County Tourism and the Sonoma County Winegrowers Commission.

The individual AVA organizations.

Their "Affiliate Members."

Sara Cummings: Best Practices, Advice and "Words of Wisdom"

Sara Cummings brings strong knowledge to SCV. But five years as Director of Communications has caused her some concern about future growth. Though SCV acknowledges many smaller wineries may opt not to seek membership, Sara maintains that it is best for the organization to not change membership rules so as to grow. Though somewhat counterintuitive, Cummings maintains that this is a "measure of success (Cummings, 2014)." Therefore, due to this success, when asked, Cummings is quite able to offer advice: if she were to advise another organization like SCV in another part of the country, what would she suggest they *must* do? Here is a synopsis of her singular "Best Practice (Cummings, 2014):"

"Collaboration is king. Organizations such as ours are definitely much better off and more efficient working together than at odds with each other. If a journalist in NYC has three different PR agencies calling him telling three different stories and, then, all the regions are calling and the vintners are calling, as opposed to one entity representing the grapes, the wines and the place, how much more difficult is that for the journalist? We are, as individual organizations, nevertheless, all syncopated, though we have slightly different branding. As the three 'umbrella' organizations, we are the example for the sixteen AVAs. Therefore, we started the Presidents' Council a couple years ago to bring together the leadership of every AVA and wine organization in the county, as well as 'Wine Road.' We meet quarterly so all of us can express and learn what each is doing and find ways to work together so as to avoid overbooking and repetition. Therefore, my one 'Best Practice' is to collaborate, above, below, and laterally."

Sara Cummings: Challenges

Sara Cummings sees growth as a healthy challenge. Therefore, given that growth, if Cummings were to advise another organization like SCV in another part of the country, what would she suggest they must strive to avoid? Here is a synopsis of her four "Challenges (Cummings, 2014):"

"Our size is a challenge! We are a big, diverse place. SCV must cover a lot of ground."

"Membership is a challenge. We would like to have every winery be a member. We have 50 percent now (250 of 500). We would love to have more. We are at about 60-75 percent of wine gallons made. We have as members Rodney Strong, the Jackson Family, the Gallo brands, Constellation, etc. We are making strides, but so many are so tiny, under a thousand cases, and our dues start at $1000 a year. We have no way to really drop a price point, therefore, our Board has decided our value is solid and we need to be 'OK' that not everyone can afford it. We seek more ways to deliver value. Wineries here have such a variety of choices to make about where they want to pay dues and what things they can support with their staff and their resources. We want to build our membership, but to change dramatically is not the solution."

"We are always seeking to find ways to add value to the membership, make it more compelling to have wineries believe they must be a part of it."

"We don't have a Direct-To-Consumer (DTC) event in our stable of events that drives people to the tasting rooms. We need to find out what we can do to address this, a DTC event. Generally, the revenue from an event like 'Passport' will pay the dues for that organization. We need to find one event that will do this for our members so new members can recoup their investment."

Sara Cummings: SCV 2014 Plans and Dreams for the Future

Thinking of the future of the organization, Cummings has two concrete hopes for 2014 and three "dreams" she wishes to share (Cummings, 2014):

Hopes:

"We could use more funding and revenue sources, so as to diversify our revenue streams a bit, that will permit us to round out our budget."

"We will continue to work on our marketing and branding to be more present because we don't have a big advertising budget."

Dreams:

"We want Sonoma Wine Country Weekend to be like 'Aspen' in terms of a nationally visible wine event and really make that event a national destination. I wish to keep 'moving the bar' and increase our visibility because, with the quality of that event, we believe it will bring recognition to our region, our chefs, and everything else."

"We don't have a DTC event in our stable of events that drives people to the tasting rooms. We need to find out what we can do to address this, a DTC event. We need to find one event that will help pay the membership for all of our members like 'Premiere Napa Valley,' a futures barrel event. That one event funds Napa Valley Vintners: they are a great example to us of a very well-run organization. And they are very collaborative with us."

"I am hopeful our wine auction will continue to grow. We doubled our proceeds last year and broke a million dollars, but we want to keep going. We want the quality of this event to reach further into our wine region more. It's a coming together of our vintner and our grower communities and the philanthropy that day. It's a fun and elegant event with loads of great food and wine. Held at Chateau St. Jean, as part of Sonoma Wine Country Weekend (the Sunday of the Labor Day weekend), we find at $500 a ticket so many choose to go to the rest of the events and not this event. Yet some might just go to this. We want to expand. We want the proceeds to better reflect the quality of what we are doing. We are on our way to achieving that."

Honore Comfort and Sonoma County Vintners: 2013 Successes and 2014 Plans

The SCV Annual Report and its Executive Director, Honore Comfort, list some of the additional successes of 2013 and the plans for 2014 not already mentioned within this Case Study (Sonoma County Vintners, 2014 A):

"We demonstrated unprecedented collaboration and teamwork on several levels in 2013, launching our brand new Sonoma County brand mark and advertising campaign in leading national publications, generating millions of marketing impressions for our region and the wines within."

SCV experienced a "record-shattering year at Sonoma Wine Country Weekend, where our vintner and grower community came together to improve the future of kids in Sonoma County through their support of Fund the Future, our multi-year initiative to improve children's literacy. Our unprecedented $1.4 million Sonoma Harvest Wine Auction revenues catapulted us into the top tier of wine auctions and charity events in America. This is the power of many coming together to say 'We Are Sonoma County.'"

"For the first time ever, Sonoma County Vintners were featured in one of two lunches during the Wine Spectator's 2013 New York Wine Experience, providing the opportunity to share some of Sonoma County's finest wines and information with over 1,000 top wine trade and consumers."

"Sonoma County Vintners partners with Sonoma County Tourism and Sonoma County Winegrowers to retain Lou Hammond & Associates, a New York public relations firm specializing in travel and lifestyle public relations. Over 220 million media impressions were generated through their work to solicit media visits and place stories about Sonoma County wines, grapes, and tourism."

"SCV traveled to Dallas and San Francisco for Sonoma in the City events, which included trade/media tastings, VIP tastings, PR events, and consumer tastings in both cities. A total of 95 VIP trade participated in seminars, with almost 600 additional trade guests attending our Taste of Sonoma: On Tour tastings. Almost 750 consumers attended tasting events in Dallas or San Francisco."

"In partnership with the California Wine Institute, SCV hosted 98 international trade and media visitors from Canada, Korea, Japan, France, Mexico, the UK, and Sweden for tastings and educational presentations. Additionally, SCV presented Sonoma in the City Canada in Calgary in October, which included trade education and tastings for top influencers, and the Vancouver International Wine Festival in February."

"SCV worked with the Wine Institute to participate in the International California Wines Summit in early October for 21 of the world's top buyers and media from Canada, the U.K., Germany, Switzerland, Sweden, Japan and China, representing California's top seven wine export markets."

"As part of our marketing program with *Food & Wine Magazine*, Sonoma County Vintners and Winegrowers and our co-op ad partner wineries participated in the publication's top wine and food events, using the opportunity to educate attendees on Sonoma County's range of terroir and wines."

"For the first time ever, Sonoma County Vintners hosted Robert M. Parker, Jr., founder of 'The Wine Advocate,' for several days of tasting Sonoma County wines to prepare a report for the December issue. He tasted over 650 wines, and stated that working with SCV provided the opportunity to discover many new producers and cover many more wines than ever before."

Case study Questions for Students:

Based on the information provided in this Case Study, complete the following seven sections so as to build a comprehensive and successful marketing plan for your chosen wine region.

1. Your Wine Region and Organization Type

Assume you are the marketing director for a wine tourism-based organization for an "up-and-coming" North American wine region. You may choose any wine region in North America and you may choose any of following three organizational types:

Destination Marketing Organization (DMO).

Grapegrowers Organization.

Vintners Organization.

Which wine region have you chosen and why?

Compare and contrast your region to Sonoma County.

How is it different? How are they similar?

Which organizational type have you chosen and why?

2. Your Organization: Organizational Structure

Based on the information provided in this Case Study, with particular attention to the sections highlighting the organizational structures of the "Trio," answer the following:

What organizational structure have you chosen?

What are the benefits and advantages to choosing this organizational type?

What difficulties do you anticipate and how will you overcome those difficulties?

What "Trio" "Best Practices" would you incorporate?

3. Your Organization: Organizational Funding

Based on the information provided in this Case Study, with particular attention to the sections highlighting the organizational funding sources and mechanisms of the "Trio," answer the following:

What funding source(s) and or mechanism(s) have you chosen?

What are the benefits and advantages to choosing this funding source(s)/ mechanism(s)?

What difficulties do you anticipate and how will you overcome those difficulties?

What "Trio" "Best Practices" would you incorporate?

4. Your Organization: Customers, Stakeholders, and Partnerships

Based on the information provided in this Case Study, with particular attention to the sections highlighting the organizational customers, stakeholders, and partnerships of the "Trio," answer the following:

Who are your customers? Explain how each is a customer.

Who are your stakeholders? Explain how each is a stakeholder.

Who are your partners? Explain how each is a partner.

What difficulties do you anticipate in managing each within your unified effort? How will you overcome those difficulties?

What "Trio" "Best Practices" would you incorporate?

5. Your Organization: Organizational Membership

Based on the information provided in this Case Study, with particular attention to the sections highlighting the memberships of the "Trio," answer the following:

Who are your members?

How do you maintain a consistent level of membership?

What is your "value proposition?"

What are the benefits and advantages to choosing this membership type?

What difficulties do you anticipate and how will you overcome those difficulties?

What "Trio" "Best Practices" would you incorporate?

6. Your Organization: Organizational Promotion

Based on the information provided in this Case Study, with particular attention to the sections highlighting the promotional efforts of the "Trio," answer the following:

How will you reach your new potential members?

How will you communicate with current members, customers, stakeholders, and partners?

How will you promote your region locally?

How will you promote your region statewide?

How will you promote your region nationally?

Will you promote your region internationally? If yes, how?

Will you promote your region internationally? If yes, how?

What are the benefits and advantages to choosing these methods of promotion?

What difficulties do you anticipate and how will you overcome those difficulties?

What "Trio" "Best Practices" would you incorporate?

7. Your Organization: Success and Growth

Based on the information provided in this Case Study, with particular attention to the sections highlighting the understanding by each interviewee of the "Trio" of the inherent danger posed by unchecked and unmanaged growth, answer the following:

If you attain the success of the "Trio" at some point in your regional marketing effort, how will you safeguard against the ever-present danger of unchecked and unmanaged growth?

What measures, policies, and organizational safeguards would you emplace so as to mediate that danger?

What measure would you employ by which to signal the onset of a dangerous level of growth?

At what point would you consider a safe level of growth and how would you mitigate against further growth? Or, if manageable, how would you measure and secure a sustainable level of increased growth?

Works Cited:

American Marketing Association. (2014). *Definition of Marketing.* Retrieved 3 15, 2014, from American Marketing Association: archive.ama.org/Archive/AboutAMA/Pages/DefinitionofMarketing.aspx

Brown, M. (2014, 1 24). *Unemployment Falls to 5.7 Percent in Sonoma County.* Retrieved 2 10, 2014, from The Press Democrat: www.pressdemocrat.com/article/20140124/business/140129768

Buena Vista Winery. (2012). *Buena Vista Today: Our History.* Retrieved 2 28, 2014, from Buena Vista Winery: www.buenavistawinery.com/about-us/buena-vista-today

California State Association of Counties. (2014). *Sonoma County, California.* Retrieved 2 10, 2014, from California State Association of Counties: www.csac.counties.org/county-profile/sonoma-county

Carroll, S. &. (2014, 1 15). *Sonoma County To Become Nation's First 100% Sustainable Wine Region.* Retrieved 2 10, 2014, from Sonoma County Winegrowers: sonomawinegrape.org/files/SCW-Sustainability-Announcement.pdf

County of Sonoma. (2013 A). *Agriculture and Tourism.* Retrieved 2 10, 2014, from County of Sonoma: sonomacounty.ca.gov/About-Sonoma-County/Agriculture-and-Tourism/

County of Sonoma. (2013 B). *Economics and Employment.* Retrieved 2 10, 2014, from County of Sonoma: sonomacounty.ca.gov/About-Sonoma-County/Economics-and-Employment/

County of Sonoma. (2004, 11 2). *Ordinance No. 5525.* Retrieved 2 15, 2014, from County of Sonoma: http://www.sonoma-county.org/tax/tot/pdf/bia_ordinance.pdf

County of Sonoma. (2014, 4 27). *Transient Occupancy Tax.* Retrieved 2 15, 2014, from County of Sonoma: sonoma-county.org/tax/tot/index.htm

Cummings, S. (2014). Director of Communications, Sonoma County Vintners. (M. R. Mozell, Interviewer) Santa Rosa, CA.

Dean Runyan and Associates. (2013, 5). *California Travel Impacts by County, 1992-2011.* Retrieved 2 10, 2014, from VisitCalifornia: http://industry.visitcalifornia.com/media/uploads/files/editor/Research/CATravelImpacts2012.pdf

Dean Runyan and Associates. (2014, 4). *California Travel Impacts by County, 1992-2012 .* Retrieved 4 26, 2014, from Dean Runyan and Associates: www.deanrunyan.com/doc_library/CAImp.pdf

Destination Marketing Association International. (2014). *About the Industry.* Retrieved 3 15, 2014, from Destination Marketing Association International: www.destinationmarketing.org/topics/about-industry

Honore Comfort. (2014). *Honore Comfort.* Retrieved 3 27, 2014, from LinkedIn: www.linkedin.com/pub/honore-comfort/5/19a/a79

Karliner, J. (2001, 3 22). *A Brief History of Greenwash*. Retrieved 3 10, 2014, from CorpWatch.

Kruse, K. (2014). President, Sonoma County Winegrowers Commission. (M. R. Mozell, Interviewer)

London, J. (2014). *John Barleycorn, Chapter 36*. Retrieved 3 30, 2014, from JackLondons.net: www.jacklondons.net/writings/JohnBarleycorn/chapter36.html

National Geographic Society. (2014). *Best Trips 2012*. Retrieved 4 29, 2014, from National Geographic: travel.nationalgeographic.com/travel/best-trips-2012/#/botw-main-gallery-sonoma_41335_600x450.jpg

Nigro, D. (2014, May 31). Can Sonoma Win Go 100 Percent Sustainable. *Wine Spectator* , p. 24.

Office of the Ag Comm, Sonoma County. (2013, 6). *2012 Crop Report*. Retrieved 2 10, 2014, from Sonoma County: www.sonoma-county.org/agcomm/pdf/crop_reports/2012_crop_report.pdf

Onit Consulting. (2014). *Onit Consulting: Bio*. Retrieved 2 28, 2014, from Onit Consulting: http://www.onitconsulting.com/?page_id=4

Perreault, W. C. (2010). *Essentials of Marketing: A Marketing Strategy Planning Approach* (12th ed.). New York, New York: McMillin-Hill/Irwin.

Pinney, T. (1989). *A History of Wine in America*. Berkeley, California: University of California Press.

Rebuild the United States. (2013). *Sonoma Renewable Strategies Conference*. Retrieved 2 15, 2014, from Rebuild the United States: www.greenjobsevent.com/bios/Karissa%20Kruse%20bio.pdf

Reilly, J. H. (2003). *IRC 501(c)(6) Organizations* . Retrieved 3 15, 2014, from irs.gov: www.irs.gov/pub/irs-tege/eotopick03.pdf

San Diego Tourism Authority. (2014). *Travel Means Economic Benefit*. Retrieved 2 10, 2014, from SanDiego.org: www.sandiego.org/campaigns/national-travel-and-touism-week/why-travel-matters.aspx

San Francisco Travel. (2013). *About the San Francisco Travel Association*. Retrieved 2 15, 2014, from San Francisco Travel: www.sanfrancisco.travel/about/about.html

Schelling, T. (1980). *The Strategy of Conflict*. Boston, MA: Harvard University Press.

Schulz, C. (2014). *The Life of Charles M. Schulz, June, 1958*. Retrieved 4 28, 2014, from Charles M. Schulz Museum: schulzmuseum.org/timeline/june-1958/

Sikara & Co. (2011, 10 3). *Real Women, Real Style: Karissa Kruse*. Retrieved 2 29, 2014, from Sikara & Co.: blog.sikara.com/real-women-real-style-karissa-kruse/

Sonoma County. (1994). *Sonoma County Aggregate Resources Management Plan and Environmental Impact Report Geology/Soils*. Retrieved 4 29, 2014, from Sonoma County: http://www.sonoma-county.org/prmd/docs/eir/gp2020deir/sec4-07.pdf

Sonoma County Tourism. (2014 C). *Annual Report 2013/2014 Marketing Report*. Sonoma County Tourism. Santa Rosa: Sonoma County Tourism.

Sonoma County Tourism. (2013 A). *Becoming a Sonoma County Tourism Ambassador*. Santa Rosa, California: Sonoma County Tourism.

Sonoma County Tourism. (2013 B). *Luxury Travel*. Retrieved 4 29, 2014, from Sonoma County Tourism: www.sonomacounty.com/activities/luxury-travel

Sonoma County Tourism. (2014 E). *Meet the Sonoma County Tourism Staff*. Retrieved 2 10, 2014, from Sonoma County Tourism: www.sonomacounty.com/meet-sonoma-county-tourism-staff

Sonoma County Tourism. (2014 D). *Sonoma County Partners - The Strength of a Partner*. Retrieved 2 10, 2014, from Sonoma County Tourism: www.sonomacounty.com/partners

Sonoma County Tourism. (2014 B). *Sonoma County Statistics*. Retrieved 2 10, 2014, from Sonoma County Tourism: www.sonomacounty.com/articles/media/statistics

Sonoma County Tourism. (2014 A). *Sonoma County Tourism - Official DMO for Sonoma County*. Retrieved 2 10, 2014, from Sonoma County Tourism: www.sonomacounty.com/sonoma-county-tourism-official-dmo

Sonoma County Tourism. (2012). *Tourism Pays for Sonoma County Vimeo 23649647*. Retrieved 3 10, 2014, from Sonoma County Tourism: http://www.sonomacounty.com/sonoma-county-tourism-official-dmo

Sonoma County Vintners. (2013 C). *About Sonoma County Vintners*. Retrieved 2 10, 2014, from Sonoma County Vintners: www.sonomawine.com/files/press/About-Sonoma-County-Vintners.pdf

Sonoma County Vintners. (2013 E). *Affiliate Members by Class*. Retrieved 2 28, 2014, from Sonoma County Vintners: www.sonomawine.com/sonoma-county-vintners/affiliate-members

Sonoma County Vintners. (2014 B). *Benefits of Membership*. Retrieved 2 28, 2014, from Sonoma County Vintners: www.sonomawine.com/files/members/SCV-Membership-Benefits.pdf

Sonoma County Vintners. (2013 A). *History of Sonoma County Wine Country*. Retrieved 2 10, 2014, from Sonoma County Vintners: www.sonomawine.com/about-sonoma-county/history-of-sonoma-county-wine-country

Sonoma County Vintners. (2013 B). *Press Releases*. Retrieved 2 10, 2014, from Sonoma County Vintners: www.sonomawine.com/press-room/press-releases

Sonoma County Vintners. (2013 D). *SCV Partners*. Retrieved 2 28, 2014, from Sonoma County Vintners: www.sonomawine.com/sonoma-county-vintners/scv-partners

Sonoma County Vintners. (2013 C). *Sonoma County Conjuctive Labeling*. Retrieved 2 15, 2014, from Sonoma County Vintners: www.sonomawine.com/about-sonoma-county/conjunctive-labeling

Sonoma County Vintners. (2014 A). *Sonoma County Vintners 2013 Annual Report*. Retrieved 2 28, 2014, from Sonoma County Vintners: www.sonomawine.com/files/members/SCV-Annual-Report-2013.pdf

Sonoma County Vintners. (2013 E). *Sonoma Wine County*. Retrieved 4 28, 2014, from Sonoma County Vintners: www.sonomawine.com/images/documents/scv_factsheetweb_pdf.pdf

Sonoma County Vintners. (2014 C). *Winery Member Enrollment Form*. Retrieved 2 28, 2014, from Sonoma County Vintners: www.sonomawine.com/files/members/SCV-Dues-Assessment.pdf

Sonoma County. (2014). *We Are Sonoma County*. Retrieved 2 15, 2014, from We Are Sonoma County: www.wearesonomacounty.com

Sonoma County Winegrape Commission. (2014 G). *Annual SCWC Sponsorship Benefits:* . Retrieved 2 28, 2014, from Sonoma County Winegrape Commission: www.sonomawinegrape.org/sites/default/files/2014_Sponsorship_Benefits.pdf

Sonoma County Winegrape Commission. (2014 C). *History Winegrowing in Sonoma County: A Brief History*. Retrieved 2 10, 2014, from Sonoma Winegrape: www.sonomawinegrape.org/files/Sonoma-County-Viticulture-History-SCWC.pdf

Sonoma County Winegrape Commission. (2014 E). *Resources*. Retrieved 2 28, 2014, from Sonoma County Winegrape Commission: www.sonomawinegrape.org/resources

Sonoma County Winegrape Commission. (2013 B). *Sonoma County Appellations*. Retrieved 2 10, 2014, from Sonoma County Vintners: www.sonomawine.com/about-sonoma-county/sonoma-county-appellations

Sonoma County Winegrape Commission. (2014 B). *Sonoma County Brandmark*. Retrieved 2 10, 2014, from Sonoma Winegrape: http://www.sonomawinegrape.org/resources

Sonoma County Winegrape Commission. (2014 F). *Sustainable Practices*. Retrieved 3 15, 2014, from Sonoma County Winegrape Commission: www.sonomawinegrape.org/sustainable-practices

Sonoma County Winegrape Commission. (2013 A). *Terroirs of Sonoma County*. Retrieved 2 10, 2014, from Sonoma Wine Country: sonomawine.com/images/documents/scv_factsheetweb_pdf.pdf

Sonoma County Winegrape Commission. (2014 A). *What Sets Sonoma Apart*. Retrieved 2 10, 2014, from Sonoma Winegrape: www.sonomawinegrape.org/story-ideas

Sonoma County Winegrape Commission. (2014 D). *www.sonomawinegrape.org/sites/default/files/2014_Sponsorship_form-web.pdf*. Retrieved 2 28 2014, from Sonoma County Winegrape Commission: www.sonomawinegrape.org/sites/default/files/2014_Sponsorship_form-web.pdf

Sonoma County Winegrowers. (2013 B). *Vine Times, Fall 2013*. Santa Rosa: Sonoma County Winegrowers.

Sonoma County Winegrowers. (2013 A). *Vine Times, Summer 2013*. Sonoma County Winegrowers. Santa Rosa: Sonoma County Winegrowers Commission.

Sonoma Wine Country Weekend. (2014). *About Sonoma Wine Country Weekend*. Retrieved 3 27, 2014, from Sonoma Wine Country Weekend: sonomawinecountryweekend.com/about-us/

US Travel Association. (2014). *Travel is an Economic Engine*. Retrieved 4 26, 2014, from Travel Effect: traveleffect.com/sites/traveleffect.com/files/states/California_UST_TravelEffect_FactSheet_50states_2014-5.pdftraveleffect.com/sites/traveleffect.com/files/states/California_UST_TravelEffect_FactSheet_50states_2014-5.pdf

USDA. (2013). *Grape Crush Report Overview*. Retrieved 2 10, 2014, from USDA National Agricultural Statistics Service: http://www.nass.usda.gov/Statistics_by_State/California/Publications/Grape_Crush/Final/2013/201303gcbnarr.pdf

Visit California. (2014 C). *VisitCalifornia*. Retrieved 2 15, 2014, from Visitcalifornia: www.visitcalifornia.com

VisitCalifornia. (2014 B). *California Statistics & Trends*. Retrieved 2 10, 2014, from VisitCalifornia: industry.visitcalifornia.com/Find-Research/California-Statistics-Trends/

VisitCalifornia. (2014 A). *California Tourism Highlights, 2012*. Retrieved 2 10, 2014, from VisitCalifornia: industry.visitcalifornia.com/media/uploads/files/editor/California_Tourism_Highlights_2012%20updated%207%205%2013.pdf

We Are Sonoma County. (2013). *Sonoma County Brand Stle Guide*. Retrieved 2 10, 2014, from We Are Sonoma County: www.sonomawine.com/files/members/sonoma-county-brand-style-guide.pdf

Wilkison, B. (2013, 12 20). *Sonoma County's Falling Unemployment Rate Buoys Economist.* Retrieved 2 10, 2014, from The Press Democrat: www.pressdemocrat.com/article/20131220/business/131229989

Wine Communications Group. (2014, 1 27). *Number of Wineries Grows to 8,391 in North America.* Retrieved 2 10, 2014, from Wine & Vines: www.winesandvines.com/template.cfm?section=news&content=127266

Wine Institute. (2013 B, 11 18). *2013 California Winegrape Harvest Report.* Retrieved 2 10, 2014, from Wine Institute: www.wineinstitute.org/resources/pressroom/11182013

Wine Institute. (2013 A, 5 7). *Number of California Wineries.* Retrieved 2 10, 2014, from Wine Instirute: www.wineinstitute.org/resources/statistics/article124

Wine Institute. (2014). *Statistics.* Retrieved 2 10, 2014, from Wine Institute: www.wineinstitute.org/resources/statistics/article697

Wong, L. (2014, 4 18). *Labor Market Information Santa Rosa-Petaluma Metropolitan Statistical Area (MSA) .* Retrieved 4 20, 2014, from State of California: www.calmis.ca.gov/file/lfmonth/satr$pds.pdf

Zahner, T. (2014). Chief Marketing Officer, Sonoma County Tourism. (M. R. Mozell, Interviewer)

About the Author

Michelle Mozell is concurrently completing her wine business MBA at Sonoma State University and her enology and wine business/marketing degrees at Santa Rosa Junior College. Her current academic focus is **the wine and wine tourism industry of Sonoma County, California, working with Sonoma State University's Dr. Liz Thach.** She has worked with wineries in Sonoma and Napa Counties in marketing, operations, production, sales, and hospitality gaining a first-hand understanding of winery and vineyard operations and securing a solid enologic and viticultural comprehension. Currently a real estate broker, her experience includes the representation and oversight of transactions involving wineries, vineyards, vineyard  estates, and commercial properties. Michelle is the former owner of four Arizona real estate brokerages and is a former commercial irrigation contractor. A retired high school history and geography teacher of sixteen years, Michelle earned her BEd from Arizona State University in 1984.